In the Cockpit!

Tales of an Aviator

Anecdotes from my life as a pilot in the 1970s and 1980s. Names, call signs, situations, events, and locations have been changed or are fictional. Any resemblance to living or deceased persons or real events is purely coincidental and unintentional.

© April 2025, Rainer R. Otter, all rights reserved by the author.
Designed: By myself.
E-mail: check-six@gmx.de
All pictures, maps and graphics without references by courtesy of author.
ISBN: 978-3-7347-0991-3
Publisher: **BoD · Books on Demand GmbH, Überseering 33, 22297 Hamburg, bod@bod.de**
Print: **Libri Plureos GmbH, Friedensallee 273, 22763 Hamburg**

Rainer R. Otter

In the Cockpit!

Tales of an Aviator

Once you have experienced flying,
you will walk the earth forever,
Your eyes turned skyward.
For there you have been,
and there you will always long to return.

Leonardo da Vinci (1452-1519)

Picture taken in Beja, Portugal 1988

Table of Contents

Foreword to My Memories

This is a very personal book. For me, the following stories are memories and experiences from a phase of my life defined by the profession of being a "Fighter Pilot and Officer" or an "Officer and Fighter Pilot." Over the course of my life, the order of significance between these roles shifted multiple times, but both professions were equally important to me. Today, when I hear or see a fighter jet in the sky, some of my memories are awakened.

> **"Not all pilots flying Fighters are Fighter Pilots.**
> **Some Fighter Pilots are driving Trucks."**

A person usually has one true witness in his life: himself - the one who lived that life. I like to compare my memories to a large bag filled with shorter or longer snippets of various experiences, thrown together in no particular order. During this period of my life, I never kept a diary, but the countless details of these memories stayed with me, captured in my own photographs. These are not my complete recollections, nor are they strictly chronological; they are snapshots of my time as a Luftwaffe Fighter Pilot.

> **"Never ask an Air Force officer if he is a Fighter Pilot. If he isn't, he'll feel compromised. If he is or was a Fighter Pilot, he will certainly bring it up on his own."**

In 1975 Werner Buchstaller, then Chairman of the Defense Committee of the German Parliament, wrote a memorable piece for the Social Party publication "Social Democratic Security Policy" (Issue No. 7/75), addressing the demands of jet pilots:

"Recently some Fighter Pilots have spoken out. What they want is simple: higher allowances. They argue that their Payment haven't increased in years. Some of these gentlemen present themselves as spokespeople for that small, pampered, and sometimes heroized group of Air Force Fighter Pilots."

Fighter Pilot never was and is not a "hero's profession." Rather, flying fighter jets, passenger planes, transport aircraft, sports planes, or helicopters is, above all, about discipline. Flying means adhering to established rules, though the limits of these rules often had to be redefined when it came to fighter jets. A mission was sometimes considered more important than the paper on which the rules were written.

Flying is about knowing and taming your inner doubts. Flying is work. Flying is also fun. Flying fighter jets is a competition. And a career shaped by the rhythm of seconds needed a counterbalance beyond the constraints of "usual" rules. We sought and found the balance in the 1970s and 1980s, never crossing the boundaries of camaraderie, military safety, flight safety, or the unacceptable. Looking back, I see the trust between commanders and squadron pilots, both on the ground and in the air, as a defining feature of that time.

The "Zeitgeist" has changed. Political correctness in 2025 is different from what it was in 1980, and that's as it should be.

However, our experiences remain in our memory within the context of the time in which they occurred. I therefore explicitly ask the readers of my memories to understand them within the context of the era in which I lived them. There are situations from the first half of my life that, later at the age of 40, 50, 60, I would undoubtedly have handled differently than I did as a young Lieutenant or Captain. We were between twenty and thirty-five years old living through the years 1975 to 1990.

More than forty additional years have since passed. To describe my memories in the language of today's "spirit of the times" would distort them. To leave them untold would not undo them.

The Luftwaffe recruitment poster from 1972 was my motivation to become a Fighter Pilot.

Hamburg Nights

There I stood in front of the barracks gate in Hamburg-Wandsbek. Until that moment, I hadn't questioned whether this was a thoroughly considered decision, but now it was too late. The motto was simple: Forward, through the large gate. I had never heard of Lala Anderson's famous song: "Underneath the lantern, by the barrack gate ...". I grew up in a small place called Winzenhohl, located in the Bavarian region, a farming village with fewer than 50 houses. Nestled in a sleepy valley, it sat in the shadow of radio waves and news from the broader world. Now, standing in front of what felt like the "gateway to the world," I only needed to pass through it. At my age of 18, that's how I saw it.

But let's take a step back.

My classmate in vocational school had been talking about his latest "conquest", describing how pretty she was. Naturally, his attention to class, as always, was lacking. "Rainer, pay attention, you'll regret not improving your language skills," my English teacher warned me. "I doubt it," I replied, thinking I had logic on my side. After all, I was still planning to take over my parents' farm.

Then I saw a Luftwaffe recruitment poster. It fascinated and, evidently, motivated me. Just three months later, I presented my parents with my application for the Luftwaffe's voluntary enlistment office, asking for their signatures. The next three days and nights passed quickly. My father signed immediately, to my surprise, given his own experiences as a wartime volunteer soldier. My mother cried for three days, and I threatened, "Then I'll just join the Foreign Legion!" The volume of our arguments rose, followed by silence. In the end, after those three days, I had both signatures. Back in 1972, at 18, I was not yet of legal age and needed the consent of both parents.

The medical examination in Munich reminded me more of a youth hostel stay than a military facility. Initially, there were no results, so I returned to back home hoping for news soon. Over the following weeks my urge to "conquer the world" and leave the village behind only grew stronger. Not long after, I held in my hands the letter my classmates dreaded: a conscription notice for the Bundeswehr (Armed Forces of Germany). For me, it was salvation, permission to escape from our valley. No friends, no sweetheart, no parents, no sibling, nothing could have held me back.

Driving a Fiat 850 with no bumpers, red rally stripes, and the rear hood propped up (as was common for rear-engine cars driven in hill climbs), I headed for Hamburg-Wandsbek. Surprised by the relatively "civilian" manner at the main gate, I found my way to the 9th Company of the

Fiat 850

Basic Training Regiment. What followed was a standard basic training, none of the extreme stress so often described. Did my comrades feel the same way? I believe so, as we were all volunteers. Each of us had a specific goal in mind; most of us already had a clear vision. It was here, that I met my first comrades who, like me, had their sights set solely on flying. We endured the service, thinking: "These three months will pass." I remember the shared joy of receiving our first paycheck: 685.72 Deutsche Marks! What better place to celebrate than Hamburg's Night Life at the "Reeperbahn"? A group of us strolled from Café Keese to the Eros Center, exploring the nightlife just like thousands of other visitors every day and night.

On the shooting range, my mess kit was filled with some kind of stew, standard field fare.

"Is this seat taken?" I asked a comrade sitting in the grass, eating his stew. The question was unnecessary, but I wanted to be polite.

"Sit down."

We ate in silence at first.

"Where are you from?"

It was a standard question; everyone knew only a handful of others, usually their bunkmates or group members.

"From Northern Bavaria."

"Where exactly?"

"You won't know it."

"Try me."

"Near Aschaffenburg."

"I know it. Where exactly?"

"Hösbach, you won't know it!"

"I do. I'm from Winzenhohl!"

"Then we can carpool home."

We made plans right there. I was to pick him up from his parents' house on Sunday afternoon. When his mother opened the door and saw me, she exclaimed:

"You're an Otter! I can tell right away because I'm an Otter by birth too!"

Is the world really so small? I had been searching for the wide, open world, trying to escape what I saw as the musty confines of the Spessart region.

Later, my distant relative, whom I had met during basic training on a shooting range, became a Phantom pilot, flying RF-4E "Phantoms" with Recce Wing 52 in Leck (EDNL).

The three months flew by. Days spent on the barracks grounds or training fields, evenings in the canteen or Hamburg's numerous obscure pubs. All of us aiming to become pilots or seeking integrated roles, such as positions in international NATO staffs, received marching orders after basic training to the nearby Uetersen base, The Air Force Language school. Back then it was still called the "Aviation Cadet Regiment," even though no aircraft were stationed there anymore, a relic from the early days of the "New Luftwaffe."

14

At the Luftwaffe language school, we took English language placement tests and were assigned to appropriate classes. My English teacher had warned me, You remember?

Our daily routine was more or less as follows:

Morning language classes. Afternoon self-study.

Self-study involved a bit of learning, some sports, trips to next towns, and occasionally meeting young women. Military duty was scheduled only one afternoon per week, and I found it more amusing than serious.

Comrades convinced me to join them in serving at the "Café Rosengarten" in the afternoons. In the small town of Uetersen, it was common for young soldiers to supplement their income with side jobs. Some non-commissioned officers even ran informal placement services, arranging shifts for "helpers" in Hamburg.

Years later, I read about the conviction of an NCO who had been involved in such arrangements. At 18, we hadn't given it much thought. Back then we didn't question an NCO's authority or the legitimacy of his actions.

Banana Steamer

At 12:30 PM, our language classes ended. That meant getting to the mess hall as quickly as possible. Before 1:00 PM students had to avoid being caught there, as the regular personnel wanted to have their lunch in peace without "these language students" around. Time was of the essence.

We often went to the mess hall in pairs at most, trying to look as confident as a soldier from the "regular personnel" and not timid like "new language students". If you got caught, the punishment was typically guard duty, preferably on the weekend. Most of the time our little charade worked.

Shovel down your food, head back to the room, change, jump in the car, and get out of the barracks. Normally the group consisted of two or three comrades, often bunkmates. From Uetersen we drove through Pinneberg to Hamburg's Free Port. The company Sergeant Major had given us a slip with the berth number of the ship we'd be working on. He had arranged jobs for us with some shipping company.

My memory tells me the second shift started at 2:00 PM. For six hours we hauled crates of bananas onto a conveyor belt. It was unbelievable how many banana crates could fit into the hold of a small freighter. The third shift began at 9:00 PM. Occasionally we worked two shifts back-to-back, finishing at 3:00 AM. By 5:00 AM, we were back at the barracks, just in time for a shower and breakfast before language class started again at 8:00 AM. In the afternoon, we'd catch up on the sleep we missed. That's how some of us earned a bit of extra cash.

Sometimes, we got lucky. When a freighter carried general cargo from Taiwan or Malaysia, all we had to do was loop a rope around the large crates and signal the crane operator. Occasionally, if a crate fell and burst open, the goods were shared among the dockworkers, and sometimes, the "banana mercenaries" like us got a little something, too.

One day, a crate burst open spilling out "shirts". Some comrades figured these shirts could come in handy. Back at the barracks, they were horrified to discover they were all women's blouses, size EU-38. The Sergeant Major would've said, "Perfect gifts for your arts-and-crafts girlfriends." That was one of his favorite lines, and it stuck with me.

Eventually the comrades got sick of bananas. Whole banana stalks regularly appeared on our barracks' windowsills, brought back by those on the night shift.

Three Options for a "Good Night Drink"

At the Flight Cadet Regiment in Uetersen, there were three options for enjoying a "good night drink" before disappearing into bed. The first was the canteen, which I can hardly recall today, except for its location on the left side of the road leading to the medical staff quarters. It didn't leave much of an impression on me since no particular memories remain.

The second option was the NCO (Non-commissioned Officer Club) club. However, we only had access after successfully completing either an NCO or officer cadet course. The NCO club reportedly had its wild moments, but it was also frequented by older NCOs, who were attending the language school and didn't particularly care to have "the young guys" around. To avoid any trouble, we didn't show up there very often.

The third and most convenient option was the Company Bar of the 2nd Company. The 2nd Company occupied several barracks buildings surrounding the drill square, and the Bar was located in the basement of my own building. What could be better than popping down to the basement for a quick last drink before bed?

Adding to its appeal was the fact that quite a few young women in Uetersen knew about the Company Bar and seemed well-versed in sneaking into the barracks, a practice that was mostly tolerated.

One memory from that time stands out vividly. It was a Friday, around 2:00 PM. Room inspections! These inspections resembled hospital rounds, where decisions were made at each bed about whether a soldier could go home for the weekend. The "Inspection Team" usually consisted of the Company Sergeant Major (Spieß) and the Duty Officer (UvD), which was the simpler version. This sometimes led to grumbling, but we could handle that.

When the Company Commander accompanied the inspection, however, the atmosphere could become tense. His presence motivated junior officers and NCOs platoon leaders, the Spieß, or the UvD to put on their best show, demonstrating how well they "commanded" their subordinates.

It was another Friday.

Everyone was scrubbing, tidying, packing. 90% of the soldiers were heading home for the weekend. I popped into the room across the hall to find out who would be conducting the inspection. Likely just the "Spieß" they said, which meant less stress.

All room occupants had to be present for the inspection, with one person reporting to the highest-ranking officer in attendance that the room was ready. We could hear the routine unfolding: A door would open, two minutes of silence, door close... door open, two minutes of silence, one minute of shouting, door close... door open... The "Inspection Team" was approaching.

When our door swung open, the inspection began. Unexpectedly, the Company Commander was with them!

"Lieutenant, Private Otter reporting the room with three men ready for inspection!"

Uh-oh. The expressions on their faces were grim. The Spieß gave the room a cursory glance before spotting two empty beer bottles in the corner.

"What's this mess?" he grumbled. "This is a pigsty!"

The Commander didn't look happy either, likely because we'd seen him in good spirits the previous night at the basement bar.

"Open the lockers," ordered the Spieß.

One of my roommates opened his locker doors, revealing photos of his girlfriend taped to the inside.

"I know her," said the Company Commander.

"Yes, sir," replied my roommate. "That's the girl you were dancing with on the table in the Company Bar last night, Sir."

"The room is fine," declared the Commander, exiting without another word. The "Spieß" trailed behind like a head nurse, muttering: "Lucky bastards."

Staying on base over the weekend had its perks, especially for those assigned to guard duty or without money to travel home. It wasn't uncommon for young women to be smuggled into the barracks in car trunks, not just for a few hours but overnight. Bringing them in this way avoided the need for visitor passes, which would have prompted the Duty Officer to send them out by midnight. Without a pass, the issue was conveniently sidestepped.

By Saturday morning the showers were often co-ed. For the more modest women, "Gentlemen" stood guard outside the shower door to ensure their "arts-and-crafts friends," as the "Spieß" fondly called them, could shower undisturbed.

One day the entire company stood assembled in front of the barracks building for roll call, a weekly tradition the Spieß indulged in whenever company duties were scheduled for Wednesday.

I was still a freshman, unfamiliar with the peculiar customs, or, better put, the "eccentric habits" of the 2nd Company. Having just finished basic training, I expected all sorts of drills.

Standing at the front of the formation was Second Lieutenant R., holding his hunting dog, we later flew together in the same squadron.

"Company, attention!" "Align!" "Eyes left for the report to the Company Commander!"

Second Lieutenant R. reported the company present.

The commander gave his usual speech before instructing, "Second Lieutenant, take the company to the shooting range."

The lieutenant took command, ordered a right turn, and marched the company in formation toward the shooting range.

We left the barracks area and crossed Uetersen airfield to reach the shooting range. With my mind still full of "combat training chaos" from basic training, I braced for all sorts of challenges.

As we marched along a dusty forest path with trees and bushes close on either side, my mind wandered. Suddenly, the soldier in front of me jumped into the bushes.

"Must be low-flying aircraft drills," I thought. My rear neighbor whispered, "Close the gap!"

I filled the space. Moments later, another soldier jumped into the bushes.

"Don't mess this up," I told myself. "Next time there's a 'low-flyer drill, jump too."

Within a minute, another soldier two rows ahead disappeared into the bushes.

The company kept marching, gaps closing automatically. When we were about 100 meters ahead, I asked the comrade beside me:

"What kind of drill are we doing?"

"Are you that naïve?" he asked incredulously.

"The guys are waiting until we're out of sight and then heading back."

"Back where?"

"Back to the barracks - and then to the lake."

"Look at this beautiful weather. This isn't shooting range weather."

"You've got a lot to learn, rookie," he added with a smirk.

Air Force Academy

39th Officer Training Course (1974)

January 4, 1974. I arrived in Neubiberg around noon. My Fiat 850 was packed to the roof with everything I owned. My entire belongings fit in one car: military gear that took up most of the space, civilian clothes, a portable radio, books that was it. With this "household," I moved into my new quarters.

As I was studying the bulletin board, someone called out behind me: "Hey, Rainer, what are you doing here?" It was Ralf, a comrade from basic training.

I was thrilled to see him again. When we realized we'd be spending the next nine months in the same classroom, we immediately worked on getting a shared room. Before long, Ralf moved in with me.

The first few weeks at the Air Force Academy were a mix of chaos, challenges, and military discipline.

Three months later, once we had settled into the routine, some of the comrades grew bold, seeking to be something more than just "officer candidates." At the Academy most afternoons were designated for self-study. During the summer months, this self-study often found its way to a bistro in Munich or the banks of the river "Isar". A popular meeting spot was also the beer garden of the experimental brewery in Unterhaching.

The officers of the training inspection, particularly the Company Commander, a Major, often came up with motivational competitions for us. One, in particular, stands out.

During his Friday "pep talk," the Major announced a new competition for all of us: "The Best Quarters."

All the cadets of the 9th Company were tasked with making their rooms "beautiful," whatever that meant. Over the following days, during our self-study time, furniture was rearranged (beds, lockers, desks, file cabinets each rotated at least once per roommate), walls were decorated, and flowerpots appeared. Creativity knew no bounds at first.

Our room was quite small, smaller than most others. To make it feel less cramped and create a cozy atmosphere, we had to optimize the space. We pushed desks against the walls and shoved the beds together to make more room. Filing stands were repurposed as nightstands, books were neatly arranged on a small bookshelf we'd brought along.

We needed something decorative for the walls. It had to be a little original but still "beautiful." One afternoon, Ralf drove to Munich and picked up two posters from a shop, one of attractive girls on the beach under palm trees, and another of a Model lounging in a hammock. Ralf insisted our room should neither look like an Armed Forces Depot nor a garden shed.

Two weeks later the room inspections were scheduled, along with the announcement of the "Best Quarters" winner.

Naturally, the inspection was led by the Company Commander accompanied by all four classroom leaders and, as always, the Spieß, the Sergeant Major.

A short knock, the door opened. No superior waited for an invitation, only subordinates did. The Company Commander and his entourage stood in our room.

"Officer Cadet Otter reporting the room occupied by two men, cleaned, ventilated, and ready for inspection."

"At ease!" the Company Commander replied.

Hands behind his back, he began to pace the room. His entourage stood at the doorway. He examined the desks, the beds, the walls first the left wall, then the one behind the beds. All heads turned to the right, to the wall behind the desks, then back to the left, then to Ralf, and finally to me.

The "Boss" turned to his classroom leaders, then eyed the Spieß, and finally returned his gaze to Ralf. The Commanders complexion darkened.

The veins in his neck and temples swelled, his mouth twitched, and his eyes narrowed into piggy little slits. A "chilling fury" filled the room.

"This is not an officer cadet's quarters!" he bellowed.

"Unbelievable! Sodom and Gomorrah! Never before has there been a double bed in a barracks!"

"And these naked women - they come off the wall!"

"Why?" Ralf asked.

The Company Commander ignored the question, continuing his tirade.

"What were you thinking?"

Murmurs of agreement came from his entourage.

"Cadet, report to my office at 2:00 PM," the Major ordered.

"Yes, Sir," Ralf replied.

I cautiously asked, "Should I report as well, Sir?"

"No." Then I won't.

The Commander stormed out of the room as if fleeing the scene, followed by his officers and, finally, the Spieß.

"What's that idiot's problem?" Ralf asked after the door shut, as we sat back at our desks.

"No idea, but he clearly doesn't like our posters or the double bed giving us more space."

"Cultural Philistine. Concrete head…"

It wasn't until later that I understood the Commander's reaction. He was a soldier through and through; he couldn't have reacted any differently.

Ralf returned from the Company commander's office that afternoon in a rage.

"He's completely lost it! This is unacceptable… that idiot!" Ralf ranted for a while before calming down.

"What did he want?" I finally asked.

"An officer cadet doesn't put naked women above his bed."

"And he said any officer behaving like that is asocial."

"He can't treat me like this!"

"Relax," I tried to reassure him. "He'll forget about it soon enough."

But Ralf wasn't one to let it go.

The following Monday I returned to find him taking the posters down.

"Are you nuts?" I asked. "I paid for those, too. They're staying."

"They're going back up," he assured me. "But first, I'm taking them to the Regimental Commander."

"You're kidding."

"I've already made an appointment."

"Bold move, Ralf. Let's hope this doesn't backfire."

Ralf rolled the posters up and marched off to see Colonel H., the Regimental Commander. Thirty minutes later, he returned.

"The posters go back up," he announced. "I told the Colonel I'm engaged to the daughter of a Lieutenant Colonel. It's almost true, we went for dancing at 'Yellow Submarine' in Munich all the time."

We are ready for the "dance class".

"And I added that accusing me of asocial behavior' would extend to my fiancée, an officer's daughter, and her father, a Lieutenant Colonel at the Secret Service."

That was a charge no old-school Colonel could let slide.

I suspect our Company Commander got a dressing-down. From that day on, Ralf had the Regimental Commander's favor, and the posters stayed on the wall until we successfully completed the Air Force Academy.

Apparently, the Colonel liked the glamorous girls more than the Major, who took his role as a disciplinarian far too seriously.

We separated the beds again, though.

Why the blame for our decorations fell entirely on Ralf and not on me, I'll never know. Ralf never held it against me.

"Fürsty" Airbase

The Legendary Training Facility.

Known as the "Cradle of the German Air Force" legendary training facility was synonymous with the beginning of military aviation for us. It was the start of our aviation journey, the dream of every young officer with whom I began flight training. Finally, we heard the roar of jet engines at an airfield, our daily life suddenly felt much more alive.

Before the flying began, we had to tackle the theory, referred to as "Academics." This meant studying, studying, and more studying. The focus shifted from topics like leadership, political science, inner guidance, and air warfare to subjects like aircraft technology, navigation, instruments, aviation law, and emergency procedures.

Heuer Air Force Pilot Watch

Survival Knife

But the most exciting part wasn't the new subjects it was the flight suit! Receiving our special aviation gear was a milestone: orange flight suits, gray leather jackets, flight gloves, Puma knives, aviator sunglasses, fire-resistant undergarments, yellow silk scarves, and flight boots.

The flight suits were bright orange-red, signaling to everyone: "Attention, flight personnel." The distinction from the "pedestrians" was complete. While there weren't many young women on base during the day to impress, the transformation from "pedestrian" to "pilot trainee" was unmistakable, not just because of the bright orange suit but also in our self-perception. Many young lieutenants were barely recognizable, filled with newfound confidence.

What a feeling it was to put on the flight suit in the morning, stow the Puma knife in the right thigh pocket secured with an elastic strap, throw on the leather jacket, and head to the staff building for breakfast. There, over coffee, you'd meet the other aspiring pilots.

For weeks this "prologue" played out: morning classes, afternoon self-study, and frequent walks to the airfield fence to glimpse the planes parked just beyond it. There they stood Piaggio P.149D trainers, G.91 "Ginas," T-33s, and even the old "Noratlas" still in service in 1974. Guest aircraft, planes not part of the Weapon School 50 also landed here including F-104 Starfighters, F-4F/RF-4E Phantoms, Mirages, and many other types.

Yet the road to our ultimate goal was paved with more theory. Morse code lessons were particularly tedious. Memorizing the Morse alphabet was one thing; transcribing Morse signals was far harder. Our instructors gave us German mnemonics to help:

.-.. ("I love you") = "L"
..-. ("F" you") = "F"

The First Flight

November 14, 1974. It was a bright, warm late autumn day. We had spent the past two days on the so-called "Flight Line," the active airfield. The days were filled with procedures with such as emergency protocols, starting procedures, and preflight checks. We quizzed each other endlessly on what we'd learned. Meanwhile, we decorated our "flight room" with a personal touch. Unlike at the Air Force Academy, there was no competition this time. We painted characters like Asterix, Obelix, and Miraculix on the walls, a nod to the popular comic series of the time. Our "artists" were unstoppable.

With parachute and headphones in hand, I walked alongside my flight instructor, First Lieutenant K., to my first flight. I was nervous to my core. My instructor strode purposefully across the Flight Line, where a row of Piaggio P.149Ds awaited in front of the training hangar, known as the "Zulu Hangar".

Deep breath. Ten meters to aircraft 91+56. "I hope she's ready to fly," I thought. Nearby, other trainees practiced preflight checks, familiarizing themselves with the cockpit on the ground while waiting for their turn to fly.

I climbed onto the left wing, opened the canopy as we'd practiced, and placed my parachute and headphones on the seat. Everything had to be done by the book during the familiarization phase.

The first checks began. Ensuring the parking brake was set, conducting a "walk-around" to confirm that all maintenance panels were closed, tires had enough tread, and the markings on the tires and rims aligned. The propeller had to spin freely, and the oil level needed to be sufficient.

Jet pilots jokingly referred to the walk-around as "Kick the tire, light the fire," but I didn't know that at the time.

My flight instructor seemed emotionless, as though he'd rather have called it a day than flown with me. A ground crew member helped us strap in.

"Fuel valve open, ignition set, parking brake engaged, flaps to half, throttle to start, ignition switch pressed," and the propeller roared to life, sending a gust of wind through the cockpit.

The First Lieutenant turned on the radio and contacted the tower.

"Fürsty Tower, Rainbow. Good morning, taxi."

"Rainbow, taxi to Runway 09 right, 1025 mbar."

Piaggio 149D

"So, let's go!" Said my instructor suddenly more animated.

"Feel the throttle and stick to see how they respond," he instructed. I was allowed to control the rudder pedals, which steered the nose wheel and operated the brakes on the ground. My instructor handled the throttle.

We taxied to the take-off position of Runway 09, completing the final checks: "Flaps set, trim adjusted, feet on the brakes."

He pushed the throttle forward, and the aircraft began to vibrate, a sensation that resonated through my entire body.

"Cylinder head temperature, max 245°C. Oil pressure, OK. RPM 3400. Brakes off."

The propeller dug into the air, pulling us forward. The aircraft accelerated, wanting to veer off course. I overcorrected with the rudder pedals, my movements timid compared to the firm corrections from my instructor.

At 70 knots, he pulled back on the stick, and suddenly, we were airborne.

The vibrations eased into a hum as he retracted the landing gear. The whine of the gear motor startled me, and the gear locked into place with a loud "bang."

We climbed steadily, passing 500 feet above the ground, 2300 feet on the altimeter. Beneath us, the runway, meadows, and fields stretched away. The higher we climbed, the calmer the Piaggio became.

At 3300 feet, we leveled off, cruising at 120–130 knots. My instructor guided me through basic maneuvers: turns, maintaining altitude, rolling out on a set heading, climbing to 3800 feet, and descending back to 3300.

"You have it."

"I have it."

These words signaled the handover of control. The 45 minutes of training flew by quite literally.

On our way back to the airfield, the chatter on the radio added humor to my nerves. "Rainbow, did yours puke?" asked one instructor. "No, did yours?" "Yeah," came the reply. "Now mine's throwing up too!"

These comments made my stomach churn. Thankfully, the approach to the runway distracted me.

My instructor called out every step: "Left-turn to 273°, throttle back, gear down, flaps to position III, right turn, nose down, not too steep, keep turning, nose down."

The runway appeared ahead of us. The descent felt steep, and I struggled to process all the sensations. The Piaggio bounced slightly as it landed, the nose wheel still in the air.

"Ease the nose down," my instructor instructed, taking over to ensure a safe landing.

After rolling back to our parking spot, we completed the post-flight checks. The so-called "Dollar Ride" was done. From now on, we would receive a flight pay supplement.

As I climbed out, I noticed a few comrades with "doggy bags" in hand, filled puke bags. Aircraft mechanics were always relieved when new trainees completed their first flights without leaving a mess in the cockpit. Those who did have to pay a case of beer as a penalty, a customary price.

Lieutenant

Things happened fast.

Promotions became more frequent occasions for celebration. Those who completed the Air Force Academy as Cadets (Fahnenjunker), were promoted to Ensign (Fähnrich) three months later, followed by another promotion to Second Lieutenant (Leutnant) after another three months. Our crew included several lateral entries, non-commissioned officers (NCOs) in training to become officers  (OA, jokingly referred to as "ohne Ahnung," or "without a clue"). Among them were Staff Sergeants (Stabsunteroffiziere OA) and Senior Sergeants (Oberfeldwebel OA), which meant promotions often overlapped, giving us plenty of reasons to celebrate.

In just 21 months, one could rise from an airman to a Second Lieutenant (pay grade A9), a career path that was financially appealing as well.

One important reason many of my comrades looked forward to becoming a Second Lieutenant was the ability to bring "female visitors" onto the base without needing visitor passes. As officers, we could escort our guests directly without the hassle.

The mornings remained dedicated to academics: navigation, instrument systems, engine mechanics, specifically the six-cylinder Lycoming inline engine of the Piaggio 149D, meteorology, radio communication, aviation law, and other subjects relevant to flying.

Afternoons were usually reserved for flight training, as long as the weather cooperated. The "Piaggio Squadron", the 3rd Flying Squadron, was housed in the "Zulu Hangar." Here, we learned departure and approach procedures for the traffic pattern at

"Fürsty" (Fürstenfeldbruck Air Base) and emergency procedures for the Piaggio 149D.

Let's be honest, none of us could memorize all the emergency procedures for the Piaggio. Knowing a few critical ones by heart was essential, but for the mandatory "Emergency Procedures Test," we often relied on teamwork within our crew. Flight instructors were always present, except during our first solo flight and subsequent solo traffic patterns, which amounted to only three flights alone in the cockpit.

Before our solo flights we practiced basic maneuvers: straight flight, turns at 30 and 60 degrees of bank, and stalls.

The first "power-on stall" was an exhilarating experience.

"Nose up, 45 degrees above the horizon... hold it, hold it, hold it, pull the stick further back as the speed decreases..."

As the nose wanted to drop, we resisted. When the stall finally occurred, the aircraft would usually tip to one side. Since the plane was never perfectly trimmed and the aging wings had slightly different aerodynamic properties, it would inevitably break unevenly.

The Piaggio vibrated as the airflow separated from the wings, barely noticeable at first, then increasingly intense. It felt like the plane wanted to fall off to one side, but with rudder corrections, we kept it level. Eventually, the aircraft tipped over entirely.

It wasn't flying anymore, it was falling.

"Stick forward, level the wings, regain airspeed, and return to level flight with minimal altitude loss."

At the beginning of our training, this was a thrilling challenge, though it later became routine. After several practice runs, I was grateful when my flight instructor took over for a break, after all, instructors enjoyed flying, too.

Sometimes, they treated us to motivating demonstrations of maneuvers like rolls and looping, maneuver we wouldn't learn or attempt in the Piaggio.

Often, my instructor would return control to me during the approach to Fürsty, letting me fly the traffic pattern.

"You have it."

"I have it!"

The handover of control was always clear and unequivocal, any misunderstanding had to be avoided. Still, I'll recount in a later chapter how such misunderstandings occasionally occurred.

Landing practice was initially a form of drill work, what pilots called "procedural work":

"Reduce RPM, turn on carburetor heat, lower the landing gear, set flaps to half, add power, extend the flaps fully, transmit your position to the tower, follow tower instructions, correct the flight path..."

My instructor would often shout, "Too high!" Meanwhile, the tower might ask for our intentions, whether to go around or commit to a full stop landing. It was a constant cycle of multitasking, concentration, and sweat.

Success didn't come easily for me. After ten flight hours, I hit a wall. My landings weren't improving, I was unfocused, and my instructor was losing patience. It was a disaster - grade 5 (fail).

Thankfully, my instructor recognized that sometimes "a change of air" could work wonders. The flight commander assigned me a new instructor: Captain H. My progress improved noticeably.

The First Solo Flight

In my fifteenth flight hour, during a flight at Oberschleißheim Airfied, we practiced traffic patterns and landings. After my second landing, Captain H. told me: "Alright, the next landing will be a full stop."

I taxied onto the airfield after landing, keeping the engine running. My instructor climbed out, patted me on the shoulder, and said, "You've got this. Three traffic patterns solo."

I closed the canopy.

"Rainbow, request taxi."

"Rainbow, cleared to taxi runway 25."

I taxied to the runway, checking the instruments repeatedly to ensure everything was in the green: flaps to half, magnetos okay.

"Rainbow, cleared for takeoff into the traffic pattern."

As I pushed the throttle forward, the RPM increased, and my pulse rose in sync. Releasing the brakes, the aircraft began to roll.

At 80 knots, I pulled the stick back to the takeoff position, held it, and soon lifted off - alone, without an instructor. My instructor watched from the tower.

It was an unforgettable feeling. For the first time, no instructor was there to yell at me for being 100 feet too low or too high in the traffic pattern. I relished my first solo flight, even though it lasted only three laps around the airfield, just fifteen minutes in total.

Those fifteen minutes gave me a significant boost in confidence that would stay with me for the rest of my life.

Returning to Fürsty, the mandatory "solo slap" awaited. Each pilot was allowed to slap the soloist on the rear while bent over - an old tradition from WW1. Among them were men with hands like lumberjacks, and my backside ached the entire night.

I had reached the first big goal.

Tradition, in addition to the „solo strike,"
also included cutting off the tie after the
first solo flight.

Personality of a Fighter Pilot

Becoming a pilot is one of the dream professions of young boys, alongside aspirations to become a train conductor, Captain of a large ship, or a truck driver. However, reality often sets in after leaving school, and career dreams change, or, for a select few young men and women, the dream of becoming a pilot remains.

The role of a pilot differs significantly from that of a military pilot, a "Fighter Pilot." In Germany, fighter pilots are further categorized as Interceptor Pilots, Fighter-bomber Pilots, or Reconnaissance Pilots. A "Fighter Pilot" is first and foremost a soldier and officer. Among us, there were those who were more pilot than officer and others who were more officer than pilot.

I repeat my quote from the foreword:

Not all pilots flying Fighters are Fighter Pilots.
Some Fighter Pilots are driving Trucks.

Being a Fighter Pilot is a way of life: a mindset shaped by attitude, mental freedom, boldness paired with intelligence, independence, integrity, and a touch of patriotism.

What Defines a Fighter Pilot?

Situational Awareness

Known as "situational awareness" in aviation parlance, this is the ability of a pilot to remain fully aware at all times of his position in three-dimensional space, speed, and how these relate to safe altitude and attitude. A Fighter Pilot knows not only the capabilities of his own aircraft but also those of enemy planes.

In emergency situations, engine failure, onboard fire, cabin depressurization, hydraulic failure, and so on, the following rules always apply:

1. Maintain Aircraft Control.
2. Analyze the Situation and Take Proper Action.

3. Land as Soon as Possible/Practicable.

These three rules are universal for all aircraft in emergencies.

My instructor, Captain Byrd, added a memorable lesson during my Cessna T-37 training. As he quizzed me on emergency procedures before a flight, I recited:

1. Maintain Aircraft Control.

2. Analyze the Situation and Take Proper Action.

He interrupted:

"And now wind your watch!"

This meant taking the brief moment it would take to wind a mechanical watch to analyze the situation calmly and avoid panicked, incorrect reactions.

3. Land as Soon as Possible/Practicable.

I internalized this explanation, and it became second nature whenever the need arose. Even in 2006, when Taliban rockets flew over my living quarters at a camp in Afghanistan and exploded nearby, Captain Byrd's advice influenced my actions.

Fine Motor Skills

While aerial combat scenes in movies often depict brute force, the reality is that precise motor skills are critical in extracting the last ounce of performance from an aircraft. Flying in formation, in clouds or at night, with as little as one meter of separation between wingtips, amid turbulence and gusts, demands an exceptional level of finesse. The same applies to ground attack missions. Releasing bombs, rockets, or using the aircraft's cannon, referred to today as "effectors", requires millimeter-level precision.

Though modern technology in fourth, fifth, and sixth-generation aircraft may reduce the reliance on fine motor skills in weapons deployment, they remain essential in formation flying.

Self-Confidence

By this I do not mean arrogance. Too little confidence makes a pilot hesitant, which can lead to uncertainty. Fellow pilots may avoid flying with such individuals, whether on training flights or in combat missions. Conversely, excessive confidence or outright arrogance leads to the same result.

Which is more dangerous, insufficient confidence or overconfidence? A fighter pilot once compared it to drowning versus dying of thirst, the outcome is the same.

Learning Ability

Self-confidence drives a pilot to learn from mistakes. Every flight, whether a training sortie or a combat mission, is debriefed and analyzed in detail. While no pilot experiences every conceivable situation firsthand.

Emergencies, thunderstorms, lightning strikes, bird strikes, ejections, prepare them mentally for a potential "Situation X." The hope is never to encounter such a scenario, but if it arises, they are equipped to handle it successfully.

Teaching Ability

As important as learning is the ability to effectively pass on skills within a team. Whether to young pilots or seasoned "old bold pilots," a good fighter pilot recognizes their own mistakes, corrects errors in execution, and shares insights to collectively improve.

Openness

Even the most skilled, knowledgeable, and experienced pilot must work as part of a team to succeed. Handling life-and-death situations often depends on seamless cooperation with superiors, peers, and support personnel. Whether in a command post, a bunker, a ready room, or the cockpit, tact and competence are essential.

Sense of Responsibility

A pilot bears responsibility not only for himself but also for his aircraft, mission, unit, and the lives of others, both in the air and on the ground. If you've seen "Top Gun", you may recall the scene where Maverick abandoned his wingman, a critical breach of responsibility. This principle is not limited to pilots; it's a universal human value. However, in a combat mission, such failure could prove fatal.

Respect

This includes respect for the enemy, who may be a skilled warrior, whether in the air or on the ground with anti-aircraft weaponry. The "enemy" could also be the weather, fatigue, or the effects of alcohol. Young pilots are taught to view everything as a potential adversary that could kill them. A late night of partying, flying while unwell, or overconfidence, all pose serious risks.

Determination

Success as a Fighter Pilot means achieving objectives despite adversity or the opponent's skill without overestimating oneself or the team. In combat, there are no trophies for participation.

"You fight to win, and you fight to survive."

In the chapter "Fighter Pilots," I will describe how I truly experienced them.

"Selfie"

Texas

On July 4, 1975, the 199th anniversary of the American Declaration of Independence, we landed in El Paso, Texas, aboard a Boeing 707 of the German Air Force.

Our adventure in the New World began in a motel in El Paso, where my bed was equipped with a built-in "vibrator" meant to lull me to sleep. I vividly remember lying there, waiting for that damn thing to stop shaking, so I could finally fall asleep.

The next morning we flew with Texas International....

(A frequently told joke: Texas International made its first transatlantic flight to Europe. When the captain nodded off mid-flight, a stewardess came into the cockpit and turned on the light. "Who switched on that f****** light?" the startled captain asked as he woke up. "Sir, that's the breakfast light. The f****** light is much dimmer," the stewardess replied.)

.... via Dallas to Sheppard Air Force Base.

The first few days were filled with administrative tasks: moving into accommodations, getting settled, buying a car, taking the American driver's license test at the Sheriff's office (first a written exam, followed by a driving test with the Sheriff in the passenger seat), getting ID cards, opening a bank account and countless other small details.

Where would a young Lieutenant live in Texas? Naturally, in "Germantown". But not right away. Initially, we were housed in a BOQ (Bachelor Officer Quarters). After about two weeks, once the previous tenant had moved out, I could settle into my permanent quarters.

Our living area, located on the Air Base, was exclusively for bachelors. The US Air Force had taken excellent care of us. Our bungalow consisted of four bedrooms for four bachelors, a living room, two bathrooms and a kitchen.

I took over my room from Navy-Lieutenant Bukowski, who had completed his flight training and was being transferred to Luke AFB.

"Buko" was always helpful and down-to-earth, not like some of the "Salon (Parlor) Pilots," who, upon earning their pilot wings, became so full of themselves they wouldn't even glance at us "greenhorns."

Years later, I came across a fitting poem by Walter von Müller from 1934, that reminded me of this time:

The Salon Pilot
His appearance, oh, so neat and prim,
He combs his hair on every whim.
His hands, so clean, they stay away,
From engines smeared with grease all day.

Hence, why he's spotless, freshly dressed,
In a flight suit that's pristinely pressed.
The quiet skies of evening calm,
He circles, lands with such aplomb,
Enhancing tales of daring feat,
In stories made more grand, complete.

Always surrounded by ladies fair,
Who gasp and swoon while standing there,
For such he finds a great delight
The charming little Salon Knight.

A few names come to mind, though fortunately, only a few among my flight comrades fit this description.

Sadly, I never saw "Buko" alive again after we parted ways at Sheppard AFB. His final flight in a Starfighter ended tragically in the tidal flats of northern shore of Germany. It deeply saddened me. He was a "Top Gunner" and a true comrade.

Chamber Flight Training

All Air Force pilots are trained to recognize symptoms of oxygen deprivation during so-called "chamber flights." As pilot trainees, we participated in our first chamber flight even before beginning flight training in the U.S. It was conducted in the hyperbaric chamber at the Aero Medical Institute of the German Air Force in Fürstenfeldbruck.

During a simulated cockpit or passenger cabin depressurization, we were "catapulted" from a physiological altitude of 6,000 feet to 35,000 feet. Oxygen was still supplied through the oxygen mask, replicating conditions in a fighter jet cockpit. The simulation recreated the sudden loss of cabin pressure at cruising altitude, complete with a loud bang and condensation in the air. Within moments, we were surrounded by a cool mist, like sitting in a steam bath.

After an immediate "descent" to a physiological altitude of 25,000 feet (7,600 meters), equivalent to a rapid emergency descent, we removed our oxygen masks and exposed ourselves to the ambient air at that altitude. The "time of useful consciousness", the period during which hypoxia symptoms can be recognized and acted upon, such as activating the emergency oxygen supply, is only three to five minutes. During this time, each participant was asked every 30 seconds about their personal symptoms.

Hypoxia symptoms vary from person to person.

One minute after the decompression, I experienced no noticeable symptoms. Around one and a half minutes, I began to feel mild dizziness. I also noticed that

Time of Useful Consciousness	
Altitude	Time
45,000 ft. MSL	9-15 seconds
40,000 ft. MSL	15-20 seconds
35,000 ft. MSL	30-60 seconds
30,000 ft. MSL	1-2 minutes
28,000 ft. MSL	2 ½-3 minutes
25,000 ft. MSL	3-5 minutes
22,000 ft. MSL	5-10 minutes
20,000 ft. MSL	30+ minutes

pilotmall.com

my speech slowed, and the light around me grew brighter. The chamber seemed to glow, almost as if I were staring into the sun. My head felt hot, and the attending doctor in the chamber instructed me to put my oxygen mask back on.

My symptoms quickly disappeared, and within a minute, I was thinking clearly again, with everything returning to normal.

Through this exercise, I became familiar with the symptoms I could expect if I ever experienced a cockpit depressurization or oxygen deficiency caused by, for example, a malfunctioning oxygen regulation system.

The importance of recognizing personal hypoxia symptoms and the available "time of useful consciousness" in a fighter jet cockpit is underscored by Table 2[1].

Chamber Flight Training at Sheppard AFB.

When we arrived at Sheppard AFB, Texas, theoretical training, or "Academics," began. Before our first flight in the T-37 "Tweet", my first flight was on August 5, 1975, we had to undergo another chamber flight.

I already knew my hypoxia symptoms from the training in Fürsty. Although we were taught that initial symptoms could change over time, I was confident that no changes would have occurred in the short period between the two chamber flights, and I was right.

At Sheppard AFB, we were not only required to report our symptoms during the "descent" to 25,000 feet, but we were also asked to write something. I repeatedly wrote my signature.

When I first noticed the onset of dizziness, I noted the symptom. We were instructed, to put our oxygen masks back on immediately and without being prompted once we were certain of our symptoms.

The range of my symptoms mirrored those I had experienced in Fürsty, but this time, I wanted to see how things would progress. The legibility of my signature offers a clue to the outcome. The

---

[1]   Deutsches Ärzteblatt 2006; 103(13): A 851–5

doctor monitoring us placed my oxygen mask back on and set my regulator to 100% oxygen to help me regain full consciousness.

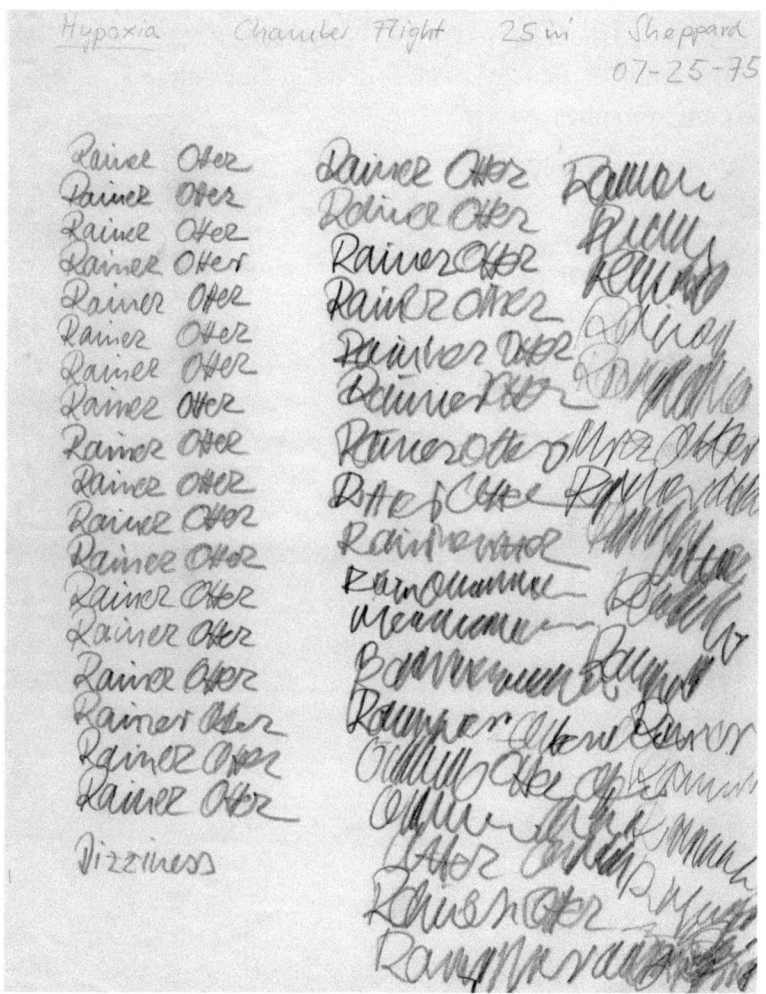

After 3 minutes hypoxia at 25,000 feet altitude..

I realized that the transition from my last clear symptom, the sensation of looking into the "sun", to complete incapacitation and

45

the loss of all awareness happened without any further warning signs. It was as though a switch had been flipped off.

This understanding proved invaluable just two years later when I experienced hypoxia at 31,000 feet in a Fiat G.91 R3.

The story of that hypoxia episode at high altitude is one I recount in another chapter.

Chamber "flight" in Fürstenfeldbruck. During the "ascent," a Bavarian comedy were always played, such as "A Munich Man in Heaven" by Ludwig Thoma. Photo: Wolfgang Capito 1977.

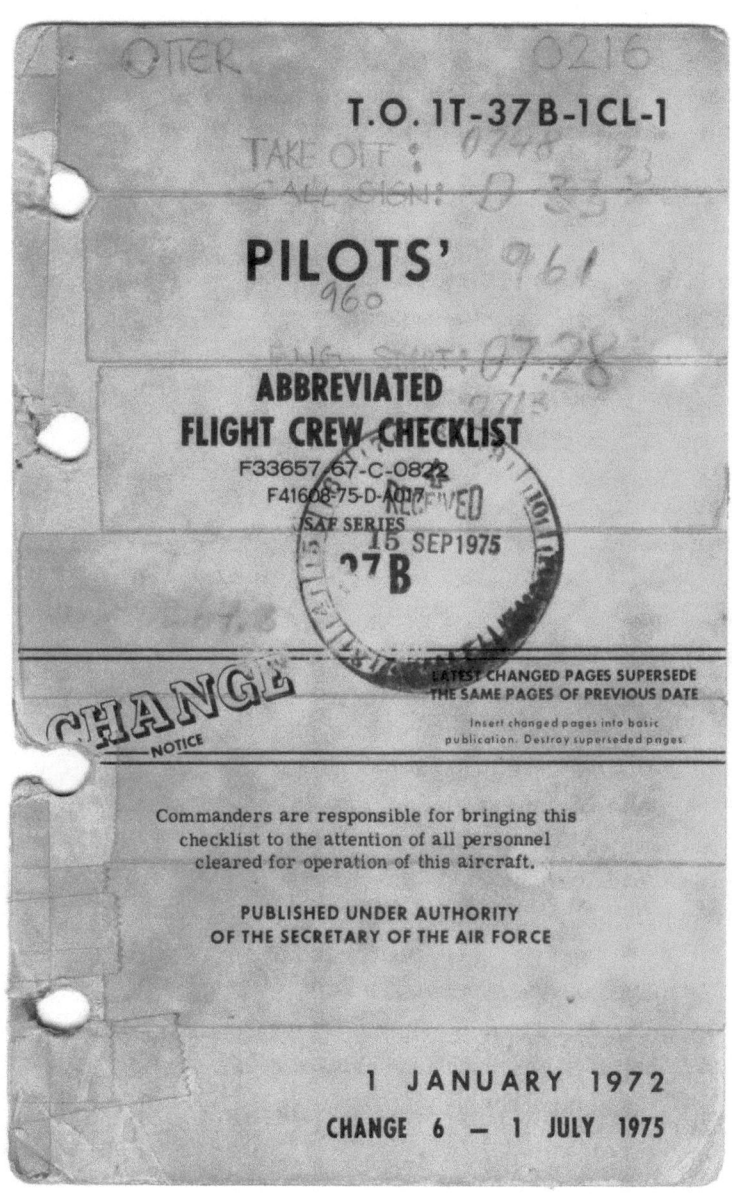

OTTER   0216

T.O. 1T-37B-1CL-1

TAKE OFF: 0748 73
CALL SIGN: D 33

PILOTS' 961
960

ENG. START: 07.28
0713

ABBREVIATED
FLIGHT CREW CHECKLIST

F33657-67-C-0822
F41608-75-D-A017

USAF SERIES

RECEIVED
15 SEP 1975

37B

LATEST CHANGED PAGES SUPERSEDE
THE SAME PAGES OF PREVIOUS DATE

Insert changed pages into basic
publication. Destroy superseded pages.

CHANGE
NOTICE

Commanders are responsible for bringing this
checklist to the attention of all personnel
cleared for operation of this aircraft.

PUBLISHED UNDER AUTHORITY
OF THE SECRETARY OF THE AIR FORCE

1 JANUARY 1972
CHANGE 6 — 1 JULY 1975

47

"Dog-Whistle"

Flight suit, jet helmet, oxygen mask, parachute, pilot watch, aviator sunglasses - specifically a Randolph Aviator, the same sunglasses Tom Cruise later wore as Maverick in the movie "Top Gun" were the insignia of jet aviation. Equipped with these, we began our training, starting with essential theory interspersed with parasailing, simulator introductions, and a chance to sit in the aircraft itself, the T-37B, affectionately called "Tweet" or "Tweedy Bird."

Six weeks of classes provided us with foundational theoretical knowledge in subjects like aircraft technology, aerodynamics, visual flight, instrument flight, aerobatics, navigation, night flying, formation flying, and especially emergency procedures. We were

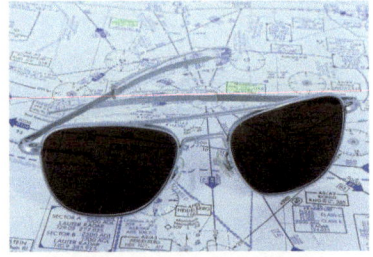

Randolph Aviator Sun glasses.

tested daily, required to memorize and recite, word for word, the protocols for system failures whether engine, radio, or landing gear. Memorization was absolute, word-perfect, including punctuation, particularly in written tests. Days were long, nights short, and every hour without sleep meticulously planned. Our days were divided into four shifts: "Early Early," "Early," "Late," and "Late Late," the latter meaning night flights.

Crew 76-09

Was there time for private social interactions? Of course. Friday evenings at "Duffy's" or the Officer's Club (O-Club) bar were popular. Back then, Sheppard AFB hosted a nursing school, where the "Ladies" attended courses lasting two, three, or four weeks. As was typical in the U.S. Air Force, all nurses held officer ranks and frequented the Officer's Club. The nurses - Lieutenants, Captains or Majors - could also be found at Duffy's, at dinner, or at the bar. On Fridays and Saturdays, there was always live music and dancing at the bar.

The nursing students rotated every few weeks, much like a "rehab" cycle.

Hearing protection, humorously called "Mickey Mouse," was mandatory on the "Flightline" and near our aircraft, the T-37B, which was also known as the "Dog Whistle." Its J69-T-25 engines emitted such high-frequency screeches that permanent hearing damage was inevitable without protection. The ground-level engine noise was painful

US Pilot watch (1975)

and genuinely nerve-wracking. Today, such an engine would be unthinkable. Though my logbook records only 135 flight hours in a T-37, I can still hear its whine when I think back to my first flights.

Special attention was given to mastering spin recovery in the "Tweet", due to past fatal solo flight accidents involving students. Spin maneuvers and recoveries were part of our training from the outset. Student pilots were not allowed to spin without an instructor but were trained to recover should a spin occur during an Immelmann turn or a looping. By 1975, we flew the modified T-37B, equipped with spin recovery strakes near the nose. These modifications were introduced after accidents where even experienced instructors failed to recover from spins, and the ejection seats offered poor survival prospects.

The "Tweedy Bird," as it was fondly called, was an ideal jet trainer but entirely Spartan. The cabin was unpressurized, limiting the aircraft to a maximum altitude of 25,000 feet. The ejection seat was a metal shell with a rocket pack, and pilots wore the parachutes, strapping it directly to the seat. With a helmet on and face enclosed in an oxygen mask, sweating began even before takeoff. The sun bore down through the cockpit like a magnifying glass, with ground temperatures of 38, 40, or 42°C translating to 55°C inside the cockpit. There was no effective air conditioning while on the ground. Sweat streamed from every pore, down the forehead into the eyes, dripping off the nose into the oxygen mask. Gloves were essential; the metal cockpit was too hot to touch barehanded. The instructor sat on the right ejection seat, eyes following every movement, ready to correct, demonstrate, or intervene if necessary.

A decade later, as a flight instructor myself, I could often sense, from slight hesitations or subtle movements, whether a student was on the verge of a significant error.

Taxiing for minutes along the long taxiways, then waiting as the fifth or sixth aircraft for takeoff, often meant a soaked flight suit before the flight had even begun. But after takeoff, as the plane climbed into the Texan sky, the air cooled, and flying the "Tweet" became a joy. It was responsive, predictable, and forgiving, tolerant of minor mistakes.

Training days at Sheppard AFB were packed from the start. By the end of the second week on the Flight Line, we logged six to seven hours of flight time with instructors. We practiced takeoffs and landings, coordinated turns, steep turns, simulated approach procedures, go-around, stalls, slow flight, spins, and emergency procedures repeatedly until corrections became automatic.

Sheppard AFB conducted up to 400 flights daily, with individual aircraft flying up to four missions per day. Despite the heavy wear on the aircraft, maintenance was exceptionally reliable. Most students never experienced technical issues during their flights. After 15 to 16 hours of dual instruction, we were deemed ready for our first solo - a jet takeoff and landing entirely on our own. On August 5, 1975, at 4:00 PM, I flew my first flight in a Jet Trainer with Captain Byrd. On September 2, 1975, at 5:07 PM, I took off for my first solo flight, mission C-2601, in a silver T-37B with tail number "005", soaring into the Texas skies. Four weeks of theory and simulator training and 16 instructor-led flights preceded that moment. Incidentally, I had just turned 21 on July 19, 1975, making me legally able to buy and drink beer in Texas.

T-37B "Tweed" 1975 at Sheppard AFB.

The first solo flight is a rite of passage, a defining moment in a young pilot's life. Mine lasted only 39 minutes - from takeoff to the third landing - but it instilled in me, at 21, a self-confidence that has stayed with me throughout my life.

After the flight, I filled out my logbook as "Pilot in Command" for the first time. Waiting for me were my fellow pilots and my German flight commander, Captain Volker H., with a hose and a "bottle of Schnapps". Though the tradition of dunking solo pilots into dirty water tanks was long gone by 1975, the bar at the O-Club hosted a modest celebration that evening. The next day's schedule resumed with my next training flight at 12:56 PM.

During the first six months I logged 128 flight hours in the T-37 Tweet. From sunrise to well past midnight, depending on the schedule, we flew and trained. Every day brought progress, shaping us as a crew without our even noticing it. Free time was scarce and spent at the Officer's Club (think "Top Gun"), buying records, or riding motorcycles through Texas and Oklahoma (again, think "Top Gun").

Punctuality was sacrosanct. Morning briefings started at 5:30 AM sharp, classes at 7:00 AM, and takeoffs at the precise scheduled times. This discipline laid the foundation for precision in flying and for the rest of my life.

Aerobatics became a staple of each flight session. Loops, Cuban Eights, Immelmanns, Cloverleafs, and Split-S maneuvers were standard. The Split-S, pronounced "Split Ess" or humorously "Split Arse" by RAF pilots during WW I, involved rolling inverted and pulling downwards to horizontal flight. Adequate altitude was critical to avoid disaster, a lesson painfully learned by early aviators.

It's not the speed that kills you, it's the sudden stop.

A "Schnapps" after the
first solo ride.

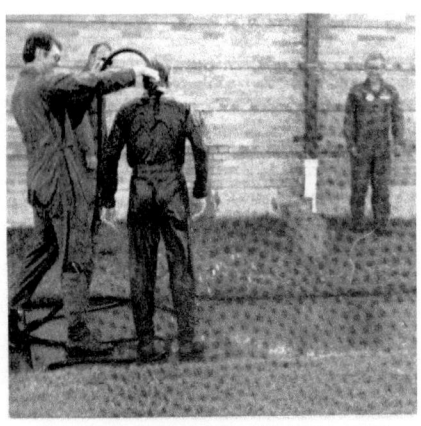

Celebrating first solo Flight in a Jet
Aircraft.

By the end of the T-37B training phase, we were recognized as pilots, though our pilot wings were only awarded after completing T-38 Talon training. From that point, we were entitled to **full pilot pay and allowances,** a coveted and symbolic acknowledgment of our skills.

An anonymous author wrote in 1917 in "Wir Flieger":

May God preserve us ground fog and pilot pay.

"God save the pilots,
Their castles evermore,
Dense fog upon the ground,
And the flight allowance…"

PILOTS'
CONDENSED
FLIGHT CREW CHECKLIST

TAKE OFF:

USAF SERIES START:

T-38A SIGN OUT:

AF33(600)39840
F41608-72-D-1959

A/C Nr:

IT. OTTER
O-0216

THIS PUBLICATION REPLACES T.O. 1T-38A-1CL-1, DATED 1 APRIL 1973.

Commanders are responsible for bringing this checklist to the attention of all affected personnel.

PUBLISHED UNDER AUTHORITY OF THE SECRETARY OF THE AIR FORCE

1 DECEMBER 1974

"White Beauty" above Dallas, Texas

In 1967 Herbert Mason wrote in his book "The New Tigers" about the T-38 "Talon": "In March 1961, the USAF received the first T-38 for operational flight service. This sleek, assertive aircraft stood on its delicate landing gear on the flight line at Randolph AFB. A significant number of Air Force officers and pilots admired the new aircraft named 'Talon.' Among the pilots was Colonel Charles E. Yeager, who had broken the sound barrier in the Bell X-1 and set the then-unmatched speed record of Mach 1.4 in 1947."

Twenty years later, Yeager wasn't looking at a test aircraft but rather the first supersonic trainer designed for student pilots (as Mason put it: "Kids"). The new training aircraft was only 1/20th slower than Yeager's record-setting speed in the Bell X-1 two decades earlier. The predecessor to the T-38 as a training aircraft was the T-33 "T-Bird." Reportedly, young pilots took too long to transition from the sluggish T-33 "T-Bird" to faster, more demanding jets like the F-101, F-102, and F-104, delaying their readiness for combat training.

The T-37B, however, was anything but sluggish. While I could understand the reasoning, it didn't diminish the joy of climbing the ladder to the T-38 for the first time, strapping myself into the ejection seat of the 'Talon', and sitting alone in the cockpit, with the flight instructor in the rear cockpit connected only by intercom.

The T-38 was designed to prepare students for their next aircraft, a fighter jet, and for achieving the desired level of "combat readiness." The flight characteristics and performance of the T-38 mirrored the fighter jets of the next generation. Even in 2020, it remained in use as a supersonic trainer: "The White Beauty."

On March 23, 1976, I flew this beautiful aircraft solo for the first time, without an instructor. Prior to that, I had completed 25 flights with instructors, nearly all with 1st Lt Liotta, who had only slightly more flight hours in his logbook than I did. After completing his training, he was immediately assigned as a T-38 instructor. At that time in the USAF, FAIPs ("First Assigned Instructor Pilots") were uncommon but not unheard of. In the Luftwaffe, such a scenario would have been inconceivable.

The T-38 was equipped with two General Electric J85-GE-5 engines with afterburners. With 2,900 pounds of thrust, it reached Mach 1.08 at sea level, breaking the sound barrier. Its climb rate was phenomenal, exceeding 30,000 feet per minute from sea level. Its maximum altitude exceeded 55,000 feet, a height we were not allowed to reach because we would have needed pressure suits above 48,000 feet. In 1962, Major Walter F. Daniel set a climb record with the T-38, reaching 12,000 meters in 95.74 seconds. This earned it the nickname "The White Rocket." Just weeks later, Lieutenant Colonel W.C. McGraw of the USMC broke that record by 22 seconds with an F-4 Phantom II.

In 1962, USAF training officials suddenly questioned whether the aircraft's demanding nature was suitable for a trainer. They selected 26 average-performing students from various training bases for a "test class." Twenty-five successfully completed the T-38 training program without accidents, significant incidents, or even a damaged tire during landings. (Herbert Mason, "The New Tigers", 1967). From the beginning, the T-38 proved itself as a superb supersonic trainer.

After the "walk around," inspecting the aircraft for visible irregularities, leaks, or damage, I climbed onto the ejection seat, strapped in, and connected the emergency transmitter lanyard in case of an ejection. Oxygen hoses and leg straps were secured, and the helmet strap tightened. The ejection handles were armed, and the oxygen system checked. Switching the battery to "ON" lit up the warning lights. Checks on the left console included:

- Landing gear doors NORMAL,
- Flight control system ON,
- Rudder trim CENTERED,
- Flaps OFF,
- Speed brakes OPEN,
- Throttles OFF.

Instruments such as the airspeed indicator, cabin pressure gauge, and accelerometer (showing "1") were verified. The onboard clock was checked for function and time accuracy. Navigation instruments were set to the correct mode, anti-collision lights tested, and radios checked. "How do you hear me?" "Loud and clear," came the response from the instructor in the rear cockpit, whom I could hear but not see.

The control tower provided the current airfield pressure, which had to be set on the altimeter to show the airfield's elevation of 1,019 feet above sea level. Circuit breakers on the right console were all verified, and the vertical speed indicator read zero. Cabin pressure switches were set to PRESS, pitot-tube heat to OFF, and the magnetic compass had to show the correct orientation. Fuel pumps were switched ON, the cross-feed pump also ON, and generator switches set to ON.

Finally, fuel gauges and oxygen levels were double-checked, and all warning lights were tested to ensure they would illuminate during emergencies. The landing gear warning system emitted its characteristic beep. Only then were the engines started using a Palouste air-start unit.

The most exhilarating moment for every student pilot was when the instructor released the brakes on the runway, pushed the throttles to "MAX," and lit the afterburners. The kick in the seat hinted at the "power" the student would soon have at their disposal and would need to control. The airspeed needle rose faster than I could think. The instructor gently pulled back on the stick, and just a few seconds later, we lifted off after less than 2,000 feet of takeoff roll.

After 24 more flights the aircraft was mine alone. No instructor was there to remind me when to retract the landing gear, adjust the flaps, or check in with the tower before entering the designated airspace. Rolls, steep turns, slow flight, Immelmann turns, and loops, I was flying solo. Alone and unafraid!

Later in the training program, 1st Lt Liotta demonstrated a "Max Performance Climb." We flew our first "out-and-back" mission, from Sheppard AFB to England AFB in Louisiana. Retracting the gear and flaps, the afterburners roared, and the altimeter needle spun wildly. At 10,000 feet, we performed checks:

- Zero-Delay Lanyard - Disconnect,
- Cabin Pressurization – Check,
- Oxygen System – Check.

Two minutes later, he rolled the aircraft slightly to the right, ending the climb, and we leveled off at 45,000 feet heading to Louisiana. "You have the aircraft," I heard from the rear cockpit. His demonstration was over; I was now in control, responsible for continuing the flight plan and landing at England AFB.

Training progressed at lightning speed, and before I knew it, I was scheduled for my first "solo out-and-back", a solo cross-country flight. Several crew members flew to Reese AFB late that morning in succession. This was the only solo cross-country flight in the program. The return to Sheppard AFB was planned for late afternoon. My flight to Reese AFB went smoothly. At Reese, like the other students, I refueled, filed a new flight plan, and spent a few hours in the Officers' Club, enjoying steak and coffee.

At around 3:00 PM, we departed for Texas in 20-minute intervals. My departure was the latest, taking off from Reese AFB at 5:00 PM.

"Solo 343 is airborne."

The flight route took me over Lubbock, Abilene, and Dallas to Wichita Falls, names very famous from country songs. The climb to 20,000 feet was uneventful. I enjoyed the solitude of solo flight, the view of the Texas desert below, and the calm voice of air traffic controllers in my headset. All instruments showed normal readings.

T-38 Formation Flight

Scattered clouds across the Texan sky were typical in the late afternoon, majestic in their towering presence. As I flew east toward Dallas, the clouds grew taller. Minutes later, they had developed into towering cumulonimbus clouds, reaching my flight level of 20,000 feet. Alone in the cockpit of a T-38, there was no instructor to offer advice. The growing wall of clouds stretched from my "11 o'clock" to my "1 o'clock" position - a full-blown thunderstorm front had developed in front of me.

"Dallas Radar, Solo 343 request FL 230 due to weather."
"Solo 343 cleared FL 230, report reaching."
"Dallas Radar, Solo 343 level FL 230."

My aircraft's nose pointed slightly above the top of the clouds ahead. "I'll easily fly over them," I thought. Once again, I enjoyed the view and the feeling of being alone at 23,000 feet over the Texas desert. It was only a few minutes later that I saw the towering clouds ahead surpassing the nose of my aircraft. "If I maintain this altitude, I'll fly into the thunderstorm," I realized. Entering the clouds was not permitted. We had only completed a few instrument training flights on the T-38 and were far from the level of proficiency required for flying under instrument meteorological conditions (IMC), let alone the experience needed.

"Dallas Radar, Solo 343 request FL 270 due to weather."
"Solo 343 cleared FL 270, report reaching."
"Dallas Radar, Solo 343 level FL 270."

Feeling calm and confident, I believed I had the situation under control again. My aircraft's nose indicated I would clear the clouds ahead. But just two minutes later, the thunderstorm clouds appeared to explode upward. The peaks of the towering clouds continued to grow rapidly.

"Dallas Radar, Solo 343 request FL 310 due to weather."
"Solo 343 cleared FL 310, report reaching."

I climbed my T-38, this "White Beauty," into the deep blue sky, hardly believing my eyes. The thunderstorm clouds ahead were rising faster than I could climb with my T-38.

"Dallas Radar, Solo 343 passing FL 300, request FL 370 due to weather."
"Solo 343 continue climb to FL 370, report reaching,"

I kept climbing, determined to fly over the thunderstorm in front of me. My engine instruments showed 100% power, and I maintained a climb speed of 280 KIAS, with a climb rate of 200–300 feet per minute. The cloud towers ahead were likely rising at 6,000 feet per minute. At an altitude of 34,500 feet, my Vertical speed indicator displayed a climb rate of zero. My supersonic trainer could climb no further without afterburners.

Suddenly, I felt very hot. At 34,500 feet, the outside temperature was around minus 45 degrees Celsius or colder, and the cockpit was a comfortable 20 degrees. But in my head, it felt like 90 degrees Celsius in a sauna. Sweat trickled down my forehead into my eyes.

The "Thunder bumper," as these massive Texas heat thunderstorms were colloquially called, could expand upward faster than a jet could climb. I had reached the "power curve" - the critical limit of thrust, speed, and altitude. My engines were already running at full power, consuming vast amounts of fuel. I didn't dare engage the afterburners because pushing the throttles into the maximum afterburner range could have triggered the following scenario:

T-38 Manual, Page 7-2:
AFTERBURNER INITIATION (HIGH ALTITUDE): Afterburner initiation attempts in the black striped area, as indicated in Figure 7-1, are not recommended. Afterburner light-off is not guaranteed

and, even if successful, may drive the engine RPM down (rollback) and possibly cause engine flame out.

In the T-38 manual's diagram, this "black striped area" began at 35,000 feet.

For the first time, alone in the cockpit at 34,500 feet, I realized: "Rien ne va plus" - nothing works anymore.

Later, I would often hear the casual saying, "They all come down eventually." In 1976, I understood that my only chance to escape the thunderstorm was to fly below it.

"Dallas Radar, Solo 343 request descent to FL 290, unable to reach FL 370."

"Negative, Solo 343, continue FL 370, we have traffic below."

"Dallas Radar, Solo 343, is a Solo student out of Sheppard AFB. I'm not allowed to enter IMC; I have to descend to avoid clouds."

"Solo 343, continue present altitude; I'll call you back."

Alone between the clouds.

By now, my flight suit was drenched with sweat. I was seated in the much-anticipated ejection seat but didn't dare push the throttles forward to engage the afterburners. Dallas Radar wouldn't allow me to descend because other aircraft were operating below me. I continued flying at roughly 350 miles per hour toward the thunderstorm clouds.

I realized I was already "behind the power curve." This concept describes the critical point where thrust, speed, and altitude reach their limits. To climb further I needed more thrust, but I had none left. The engines were running at full capacity, burning enormous amounts of fuel. Engaging the afterburners might have caused engine flame out. Every small adjustment of the stick consumed a bit of the precarious balance keeping the aircraft aloft. I was, quite literally, hanging by a thread. Even a standard turn was no longer possible because the additional lift required for a banked turn would have demanded thrust I no longer had.

"Dallas Radar, Solo 343 is leaving altitude to avoid thunderstorm, descending..."
"OK, Solo 343, descend down to FL 270, stay out of clouds."
"Roger, WILCO, Solo 343."

I gently pushed the stick forward and began a left turn to avoid flying into the thunderstorm clouds. My flight path became a zigzag through the Texas sky. The Dallas Radar controller likely recognized the severity of my situation from the tone of my voice.

With their continued guidance, I managed to navigate around the storm and land safely at Sheppard AFB, performing a GCA (Ground Controlled Approach) under visual weather conditions on Runway 33L.

No sooner had I climbed down the ladder than I was ordered to report to Major Wood, the operations officer, in the command center. There, I had to explain why I first tested the upper limits of the Texan airspace and then descended into the lower bounds of controlled airspace between Dallas and Sheppard AFB. I also had to account for why multiple passenger aircraft had to be rerouted or were unable to change altitudes to clear the airspace for a German solo student in a T-38.

The debrief ended without major consequences. After all, I had brought the aircraft back home safely.

© Markus Kutscher, Frankfurt, Germany

Shortly before completing "UPT" in 1976 at Sheppard AFB.

"The Wings"

The awarding of the Wings, in German "Schwinge,"[2] the pilot's badge of the German Air Force, not only marked the completion of "Basic Flight Training" but was also the highlight at Sheppard AFB, for which all pilot trainees strove. Jet pilots through their training with the U.S. Air Force, also earned the "USAF Pilot Wings" simultaneously. Both badges were worn by fighter pilots, with the German pilot badge positioned above the

Awarding the "Wings" at Sheppard AFB.

American wings. Interestingly, wearing the American "Pilot Wing" distinguished jet pilots from transport and helicopter pilots, who did not earn the USAF Wing.

For nearly a century, interceptor- and bomber pilots carried the reputation of being daring warriors. In popular films such as "Top Gun" with Tom Cruise, "Independence Day" with Will Smith, "1941" with John Belushi, and "The Great Santini" with Robert Duvall, a fighter pilot was portrayed as a cigar-smoking, beer-drinking, tough, lady-charming, and arrogant "hotshot" who knew no limits in flying always defeated the villains, and returned home as a glorious hero. This, however, was certainly not the average fighter pilot of the twentieth or twenty-first century.

---

2   The "German Military Aircraft Pilot Badge" was established on January 27, 1913, by Kaiser Wilhelm II.

Yet, perhaps:

"How can one be humble when one belongs to the best?"

And the "Schwinge," "The Wings," were the visible testimony of this status, comparable to the "four stripes" of a civilian airline captain.

Fighter Pilots

The ego of a fighter pilot is pronounced, but he is neither a macho type nor rebellious against authority. He is acutely aware of his vulnerability and rejects impulsiveness and resignation. He does not aspire to be a hero; his goal is for his number of landings to equal his number of takeoffs. Dignity and status were not insignificant to us, and recognition was more important than medals on our chest - except for the pilot's wings.

"Nothing makes a Fighter Pilot more aware of his capabilities and of his limitations than those moments when he must push aside all the familiar defenses of ego and vanity, and accept reality by staring, with the fear that is normal to a man in combat, into the face of Death." (Major Robert S. Johnson, USAAF)

Any fighter pilot belonged to the selected few who made it into the cockpit of a fighter aircraft. Only 10 percent of all applicants for jet pilot training met the physical and psychological requirements to be selected. From the very first moment, he is in constant competition with his fellow crew members. Air Force Academy, pilot training, and a career in the squadron, all stages of his path required him to prove himself among his flying comrades. He also knew that one incorrect lab result or one spike too many on his next ECG during a flight medical exam could abruptly end his flying career, relegating him to a lifetime of "desk flying." Despite this, the fighter pilot remains a team player.

However, the "wings" remain a deeply personal badge of ego. In my foreword, I already discussed the "Fighter Pilot." The term is inseparable from a strong sense of knowledge, independence, integrity, courage, and patriotism.

To be a "Fighter Pilot" is a way of life, not a job title.

During World War II, there was a song that became immensely popular among American pilots, capturing the stark contrast between the young pilot's expectations upon earning the "Wings" and the realities that followed. Since the 1940s, this song has been one of the classics of "Fighter Pilot Songs," particularly in Oscar Brand's 1956 interpretation on his record "The Wild Blue Yonder."

I Wanted Wings

I wanted Wings till I got the Goddamn Things – Now I don't want them anymore.
>They taught me how to fly, then they sent me off to die,
>Well I've had a belly full of war.
>You can save those bloody Zeros for other goddamn heroes
>Distinguished Flying Crosses do not compensate for losses, Buster,

I wanted Wings till I got the Goddamn Things - Now I don't want them anymore.
>Yes I'll take the dames, let the rest go down in flames,
>I have no desire to be burned.
>Air combat spells romance, until they shoot holes in my pants,
>I'm not a fighter I have learned.
>You can save the Mitsubishis, for the other sons of bitches,
>I'd rather make a woman then be shot down in a Grumman, Buster,

I wanted Wings till I got the Goddamn Things - Now I don't want them anymore.
>Now I'm too young to die in a lousy PBY, that's for the eager not for me,
>I don't trust in my luck to be picked up by a duck,
>After I've crashed into the sea.
>Yes I'd rather be a terrier, then a flyer on a Carrier,

With my hand around a bottle, you can keep your goddamn throttle,
Buster,

I wanted Wings till I got the Goddamn Things – Now I don't want them anymore.
I do not care to tour over Berlin and the Ruhr,
flak always makes me lose my lunch.
I get an erg to pray when they holler "Bombs Away",
I'd rather be at home with the bunch.
For there's one thing you can't laugh off, when they shoot your tailpipe half off,
I'd rather be at home buster with my tail, then with a cluster,
Buster,

I wanted Wings till I got the Goddamn Things – Now I don't want them anymore.
The feed us lousy chow, but we stay alive somehow,
on dehydrated eggs and milk and stew.
The rumor has it next they'll be dehydrating sex,
that's the day I tell the coach I'm through.
For I've managed all the dangers, the shooting back of strangers,
but when I get home late, I want my woman straight,
Mister,

I wanted Wings till I got the Goddamn things - Now I don't want them anymore.

In 1976, Ford Smartt[3] defined the "Fighter Pilot" as follows:

A Fighter Pilot is a phenomenon. He loves flying (single-seaters) and particularly enjoys weapon deployment, aerobatics, and flights to other countries. He has a peculiar fascination with flight

---

[3]   Red River Valley Fighter Pilots

boots, gambling, cigars (the thicker, the better), and smashing glasses against the wall. You'll find him in a sports car, at parties, or at the "Happy Hour" in the officers club. His preferred destinations include "The land of the bearded clam," Europe, and/or select locations in the Near and Far East - but not at home. He has a strong affinity for women and drinks (especially martinis). He likes "Steve Canyon", "Snoopy Magazine", steaks, and dirty jokes.

He prefers to hide in dimly lit bars, shielded by a pair of "Ray-Ban" sunglasses. He is unpredictable. Out of sheer exuberance, he shoots off flares and firecrackers, throws empty beer cans down the barracks hallway, spills drinks over plunging necklines, or behaves in generally offensive ways.[4] His favorite topics are flying, strong drinks, and women - in no particular order.

He has an aversion to survival training, scoffs at Fighter-Bomber Pilots (or, if necessary, any other pilot), detests airfield duties, and loathes long alert drills. He avoids bad weather, icy runways, radio failures, engine malfunctions, and ejections whenever possible. Water makes him sick unless it is frozen and surrounded by Scottish whiskey. He'd rather sit in front of a fireplace than push a stroller or carry an umbrella. If the word "motherhood" comes up, he becomes schizophrenic[5], and the bonds of marriage suddenly feel lackluster.

A Fighter Pilot is a strange blend. He has the nerves of a robot, the daring of Dennis the Menace, the lungs of a drill sergeant, the energy of an atomic bomb, the imagination of a science-fiction writer, the eloquence of a diplomat, immunity to suggestions, and the wisdom of a collection of disconnected, irrelevant facts. He wears the largest wristwatch, is constantly on the move, and is always looking for a good time. When trying to impress, he acts

---

[4] As depicted in the movie "The Great Santini".

[5] He's not actually schizophrenic, but he reacts that way for a few minutes.

foolishly, becomes a reckless monkey, and seems like he wants to destroy the world - and himself along with it.

What does he stuff into his flight suit? Checklists, maps, a bottle opener, a dime novel, a pocketknife, a pistol, snare traps, flares, tissues, inhalers, aspirin, cigarettes, a flashlight, more checklists, pencils, pens, flight gloves, playing cards, encrypted phone numbers, a wallet, a key-ring, his horoscope, a talisman, a "Christopher medal" or a specific coin[6], and even more useless junk, along with yet more checklists.

At home with his wife, he is submissive, good-natured, gentle, lovable, accommodating - a dream of a guy, reliable in every respect - except when there's a fight. Then he becomes an animal: tyrannical, strange, demonic, a masochistic sex fiend with no manners.

As a father, he is demanding yet tender, considerate, straight-forward, protective, visionary, ambitious, and brimming with pride over his "young fighter pilot" (and he'll never admit it or show it publicly, but this applies to his daughters too).

In the air, he is calculating and self-assured.

No one has ever accused jet pilots of being modest or humble. On the other hand, no one has ever described Weapons Systems Officers (WSOs) as particularly proud.

Has anyone ever heard the title "best WSO in the world"?

It sounds oddly different from "greatest Fighter Pilot of all time." Why was the title "Weapons Systems Officer" chosen? Perhaps to emphasize their rank within the military hierarchy - that they are officers? Jet pilots are never referred to as officers; everyone knows they are!

One day a wise father approached his young son and asked:
"Son, what are your thoughts on the future?"
The son's face lit up as he turned to his father and smiled,
"I want to be a Fighter Pilot when I grow up!"

---

[6]   See chapter "Games"

> *The sage elder shook his head sadly and replied,*
> *"I'm sorry boy, you can't do both."*

And Mel Porter summed up his life as a "Fighter Pilot" in a poem:

Because somewhere in me is still the little boy,
who wants to kick the can and write on walls,
and hitch rides on the tailgates of trucks,
and pull little girls' pants down.

And somewhere in me is still the go-to-hell Pilot,
in the go-to-hell hat flinging an aircraft,
down boundless Halls of Space,
and talking with Hands for airplanes,
and reliving the Po Delta and the Mekong Delta,
and reaching out to Touch the Face of God,
and profaning those who are tied to earth,
and pulling Girls' pants down.

And somewhere in me is the Descartes and the Sartre,
who philosophizes on the here, and the hereafter,
and the deism of all that lives and not lives,
and the beauty of sky and water and cloven hoofs and man,
and girls with their pants down.

And deep inside me there is that uncompromising realist,
who knows that this is all a terribly temporary gift
that sometime, perhaps this next second,
he must run into that last hard object,
be it the side of a mountain, the slam of a bullet,
or that massive grasp of a giant's hand on a faltering heart.

When that time comes, if there is one thing to remember,
it will be that sweet memory that transcends them all,

the little boy, the go-to-heller, the philosopher, the realist;
it will be the ineffably beautiful picture
of a girl. . .with her pants down.

The pilots in a fighter-bomber squadron of the 1970s and 1980s were a motley crew, as if they had been randomly plucked from civilian life. It was a time when many of the "old pilots" came from the ranks of non-commissioned officers - lateral entrants without high school diplomas. Officers with university degrees were the exception back then; today, they are the rule. Educational backgrounds were far from uniform.

There was the young First Lieutenant who already dreamed of a career as a Three-Star General and worked toward that rank every single day. Then there was the Captain, who became a fighter pilot in the Air Force after high school and only wanted to fly. There was the Major who spent his annual vacation in India at a Hare Krishna Club. I remember the young First Lieutenant who liked to eat his "Baby fruit purée" between flights. There were the diary keepers and the "Hustler" readers. There were the successful types and the less successful ones, the introverts and the loud ones, the adventurers and the bookworms.

Yet, there were commonalities. Most pilots were in their mid-twenties to mid-thirties. A pilot who crossed the age of 35 was considered an "old man." Combat pilots over the age of 41 were unheard of. Most pilots left the Air Force by the time they turned 40, retiring from active duty. Those few who stayed moved to other roles, often at NATO or in command offices, before their 40th birthday. Most were family men, while a few remained "eternal bachelors."

But one trait was shared by all: they were men of action. The "Yogi" and the "bookworm," the "career-oriented" and the "fruit puree enthusiast," the "diary keeper" and the "Hustler picture viewer" - each one strapped onto an ejection seat with enthusiasm, donned a helmet with an oxygen mask over mouth and nose, and taxied toward the runway. With the thunderous roar of engines, he would take off in his multi-million-dollar aircraft into the clear blue sky or into low-hanging, gray rain clouds to carry out his assigned mission.

He would lead a two-aircraft element through the clouds or the night, flying wingtip to wingtip, often with only a few feet distance between them, glued to the leader's wing. He would guide a four-aircraft formation to a bombing-range for bombing or rocket practice. He might coordinate twelve aircraft in a simulated attack on an enemy airfield. After takeoff, he might plunge into a snowstorm, only to land 1,500 kilometers away two and a half hours later on an airfield in southern France under a clear blue sky at 25 degrees Celsius.

He would confide in his diary or a squadron mate at the bar about the emergency measures he had taken when the red "Warning" or yellow "Caution" lights or both, lit up on his console. He would recount how he landed without flaps or when his landing gear failed to deploy. One might boast about his gunnery results, while another would say nothing about losing cabin pressure.

But all these pilots, however different they were, turned their words into action the moment they stepped into a cockpit.

There were evenings when shot glasses flew to the ceiling, fireworks were lit in July and tossed under tables, pianos in the officers mess were burned, double entendres were shared, and bawdy songs were sung. But by the next day, every one of them was back in the cockpit, leading a four-ship formation to simulate tank attacks on a training ground or flying as "Number Two" above the clouds to practice air combat.

Every pilot was a man of action, and each day brought new deeds. Their hands were encased in white goatskin gloves. The left hand ruled the engine; the right-hand governed life and death, the control stick, and the trigger.

It took time to make friends with some of these men. Young pilots first had to prove themselves, demonstrating they could be trusted and that others could entrust their lives to them. A pilot with three years in a squadron was "light-years" ahead of a newcomer. A pilot with ten years of flying experience, typically in his early to mid-thirties, was considered "infinitely experienced." Only a few were exceptions to this. Over time, young pilots learned that Lieutenant M. had once flown through trees and narrowly avoided a crash that Major L. had taken a ricochet through his cockpit canopy during air-to-ground gunnery, or that Captain H. had collided with a stork during low-level flight, severely damaging his aircraft and forcing an emergency landing.

All pilots shared a profound respect for the luck they needed to survive and for the technology that usually worked but occasionally failed. But showing humility - that was something none of them wanted or could do.

It is undoubtedly difficult for young men to show humility when they are among the best.

**There are old pilots, and bold pilots,
but no old bold pilots.**

Afterthought:

"The jerk rate among pilots was absolutely zero."
Jo Rammer, Starfighter Pilot[7]

---

[7]   „Mach 2" by Rolf Stünkel, Page 111.

Gina

At the end of my jet pilot training, I volunteered for the Fiat G.91 because my flight instructor, Captain H., a former pilot FBW 41, had painted an enticing picture of the "Fighter Bomber Wing 41" (LeKG 41). However, since a pilot couldn't be sent alone to retrain on the G.91 at "Fürsty," the squadron commander quickly ordered another flight student to accompany me. My crew mate, Lieutenant G., felt cheated out of his longer stay in the United States because of this. Like me, he had been assigned to Luke AFB, Arizona, to fly the F-104G "Starfighter." He never fully forgave me for the consequences of my decision.

Such is the harshness of a soldier's life.

The retraining and "Europeanization" - adapting to the tight European airspace, European weather conditions and weapons training were the next challenges.

The Fiat G.91 was affectionately called "Gina" in both the German and Portuguese Air Forces. In the Italian Air Force, it was known as "Gigletto."

Fürstenfeldbruck, known as "Fürsty" or, in "American English," "Fursty," became my home airfield for the second time, and I would return there twice more as a pilot, assigned to the Fighter Bomber Wing 49.

A Brief History of the G.91[8]

The Fiat G.91 "Gina"[9] was procured almost simultaneously with the F-104G "Starfighter."

The procurement of the Fiat G.91 was based on a NATO requirement from the early 1950s, predating Germany's NATO membership. The experiences of the Korean War formed the basis for developing a new aircraft that would be introduced across all NATO member states.

The requirement described the desired aircraft as follows: It was to be a light and simple standard aircraft for close air support of ground forces, suitable for reconnaissance and, to a limited extent, for front-line fighter tasks. It would also serve as a combat trainer across all NATO air forces. The machine was to be technically, logistically, and operationally simple yet efficient in use. It was even intended to have the potential for deploying nuclear weapons in the future. The defensive component of the aircraft was defined as its ability to protect itself from enemy nuclear attacks.

The aircraft was required to take off and land from makeshift airfields and, if necessary, operate from concealed forest locations near the frontline to support ground forces effectively. This flexibility could only be achieved with minimal maintenance requirements, meaning the Fiat G.91 was to have only the most essential equipment.

The tender ended in 1958, resulting in what could be described as a "typical alliance compromise." While the goal was to procure an aircraft for all NATO states, the British and French never seriously considered adopting a foreign model alongside their own designs. Competing models included the French "Etendard"

---

[8]   Information on the procurement of the Fiat G.91 comes
       from the book *Die Luftwaffe 1950-1970* by Oldenbourg
       Verlag.

[9]   The nickname "Gina" refers not to the "G" in the aircraft's
       designation but to actress Gina Lollobrigida.

and the "Taon." The British proposals, the "Gnat" and a lightweight version of the "Hawker," were withdrawn.

In November 1958, Germany decided to procure the Fiat G.91. A total of 344 G.91 R3 (single-seaters) and 66 G.91 T3 (two-seaters) were ordered. However, by the 1960s, budget cuts reduced the number of squadrons the Air Force could establish as initially planned.

Unexpectedly, an additional 50 G.91 R4 aircraft, ordered under a U.S. aid program for Greece, ended up on German airfields. The Greek Air Force did not want the Fiat G.91. This increased the number of aircraft assigned to the G.91 squadrons, while the rest were stored. Later, as part of a compensation agreement for financial obligations tied to the Beja Air Base in Portugal, 40 G.91 R4 aircraft were offered to Portugal and quickly delivered.

Portugal immediately deployed the G.91s, which they kept in service at Montijo until 1993, during the independence wars in Guinea-Bissau and Mozambique.

For the German Air Force planners, the electronic equipment of the new aircraft was a decisive factor. Expectations for the capabilities and electronics of the F-104G were exceptionally high, but for the G.91, they demanded the exact opposite: maximum simplicity, no complex devices. The Air Force leadership deemed features like Identification Friend or Foe (IFF), high-resolution reconnaissance equipment, or instruments for instrument flight unnecessary, arguing that such equipment would be ineffective during low-level flight.

In contrast, the Federal Office for Defense Technology and Procurement (BWB) demanded more extensive equipment than Fiat originally offered. Fiat implemented these demands but refused to guarantee operational reliability for the resulting design.

The Fiat G.91 was ultimately equipped with a radio compass, a gyro platform (PHI) with a flight path computer that was rarely used in flight, a simple gunsight, three cameras, and two 30mm DEFA cannons.

The Air Force also considered equipping the G.91 with nuclear capabilities, testing a prototype with the U.S. Mk-57 nuclear bomb. However, the simple technology of the Fiat G.91 presented challenges in deploying nuclear weapons from makeshift airstrips, such as highway segments, on near-front battlefields. The NATO strategy shift from "Massive Retaliation" to "Flexible Response" ultimately ended these plans.

Thank God for that!

Fiat G.91 R3 of LeKG41

Waffenschule der Lfv 50

Urkunde!

Dem
Lt Rainer Otter

wird hiermit bescheinigt, daß er die Waffenausbildung zum

Flugzeugführer

auf Fiat G-91   erfolgreich beendet hat.

Waffenschule a Lfv. 50
Fürstenfeldbrück, den 22.Sept. 1977

Staffelkapitän   Kommandeur   Einsatzstabs-Ufz.

Certificate for successful conversion to the Fiat G.91

First Solo Flight in a Single-Seater

Until then, my solo flights had always been solo missions in a two-seater training aircraft. But on March 7, 1977, I took off for the first time in a "single-seater." On the flight line, the G.91 R3 with the tail number 30+80 was waiting for me.

The briefing with my flight instructor was similar to the previous ones, but this time, my instructor thoroughly emphasized the differences between the two-seater and the single-seater.

For the first solo flight in the Fiat G.91, the instructor would fly alongside the student in the so-called "chase position," ensuring the flight was conducted safely and offering assistance in the air if necessary.

DATE 19.77	DEPARTURE & ARRIVAL		AIRCRAFT		NO. OF TAKEOFFS		NO. OF LANDINGS		REMARKS, MANEUVERS, SAFETY PILOT, PLACE/TYPE OF IFR APPROACH, ETC.
	FROM	TO	MAKE & MODEL	IDENT. MARK	D	N	D	N	
MÄRZ 02	EDSG	EDSF	G91/T3	3450					ET-5 MAJ. WOZNIK
MÄRZ 03	EDSF	EDSF	G91/T3	3402					ETI-3 MAJ. WOZNIK
MÄRZ 07	EDSF	EDSF	G91/R3	3080	1		1		TC-5 MAJ. WOZNIK/SOLO -CHASE
MÄRZ 07	EDSF	EDSF	G91/R3	3070	1		1		TC-7 SOLO
MÄRZ 10	EDSF	EDSF	G91/R3	3035	1		1		TC-8 SOLO
MÄRZ 10	EDSF	EDSF	G91/T3	3422					TI-1 HPTM. HELLWIG
MÄRZ 11	EDSF	EDSF	G91/T3	3416					TI-2 HPTM. SCHREIBER
MÄRZ 14	EDSF	EDSF	G91/T3	3442					TI-3 HPTM. BAUMANN
									PAGE TOTAL
I CERTIFY THAT THE ENTRIES ON THESE PAGES ARE CORRECT:									TIME BROUGHT FORWARD
PILOT'S SIGNATURE _____									TOTAL TO DATE

After a detailed discussion of the mission, we headed to the R&S shop to collect our life vests and helmets. On that spring day, we walked from the squadron building to the aircraft parking area. I conducted the necessary external checks, the "walk-around check." The ground crew handed me a perfectly maintained aircraft.

I reviewed the entries in the aircraft logbook, the "Form 781", signed it, climbed the ladder into the cockpit and had the "First Technician" assist me in fastening the harness. Finally, the leg straps were secured around my calves. These straps were designed to pull the legs back against the ejection seat during an ejection, minimizing the risk of injury.

Helmet on, oxygen hose connected, and a glance at the ground crewman, who gave me a thumbs-up.

I proceeded with the pre-engine-start checks:

-Ignition and Start c/b–in
-Battery and Generator switches – ON
-Voltmeter – minimum 24 V
-Fire and overheat circuit – Check
-All warning and indication lights– Press to test
-Landing gear indication – Three wheels
-Landing gear horn button – Press to test
-HE ignition switch – NORMAL
-Airstart ignition button – Press (listen for sparking - you could hear the ignition spark)
-Fuel booster pump switch – ON
-Throttle – Full OPEN, then IDLE
-Starter Button – Depress for 2 sec, check out after 30 sec

The starter cartridge ignited, releasing a thick gray puff of smoke from the left side of the aircraft. The engine spooled up, settling at 35% power output, with the exhaust gas temperature below 700º C. Everything was in the "green."

G.91 engine start. Photo from the "Wache collection".

"NOCONA cleared to Taxi RWY 27."

I signaled the ground crewman to remove the chocks. He gave me another thumbs-up, and I taxied to runway 27.

At that moment, a new chapter began - a thrilling journey as a single-seat pilot in the German Air Force. My pilot training was officially complete, even though we were technically still "retraining" on the Fiat G.91 weapons system. We were, however, already "men with a license to fly."

A Curious Keepsake

I still have a small memento on my desk - the "Cross-Country Toolkit" for the G.91 "Gina."

Cross-Country Toolkit

A tool was not necessary for changing the starter cartridge. The brake chute could also be replaced without any aids. Even refilling the oil level required no tools - except for the "thin screwdriver" from the toolkit, which was used to puncture the oil can. During international flights, we were always provided with a can of oil, and checking the oil level was mandatory before every flight.

The flat side of the screwdriver was essential for opening and closing the fuel caps (a total of four). As for working on the battery, which was accessed from below, no tools were needed at all.

G.91 R3, tail number 40+80, with which I completed my first solo flight in a single-seater, is now displayed in Horta do Douro, Portugal. Photo Peter Zucht

Low-Level Navigation in a Single-Seater

The objective of low-level navigation was to fly from point A to point B, then to point C, and so on. Along the way, there would typically be a target for attack - often a second target as well - and the final "point" would be the airfield where the pilot would land.

Low-level route in Portugal, navigation template for low-level flight planning with the Fiat G.91

So far, so good. Let's take a closer look at how low-level navigation was conducted during an era when GPS had not yet been invented, Google Maps didn't exist, and navigation relied solely on maps, compass, and clock.

The Fiat G.91 had neither radar nor an onboard computer, and when the guns were armed, the TACAN navigation system had to be removed. Navigation was essentially no different from 1914, except we were now flying primarily at low altitudes - 500 or 250 feet - and at speeds of 360 to 400 knots, approximately 666 to 740 km/h.

Low-level flight was indispensable during the Cold War to evade enemy radar, ensuring that our aircraft were detected as late as possible.

The survival formula for fighter-bomber pilots was:

"The faster and lower you fly, the higher your chances of survival."

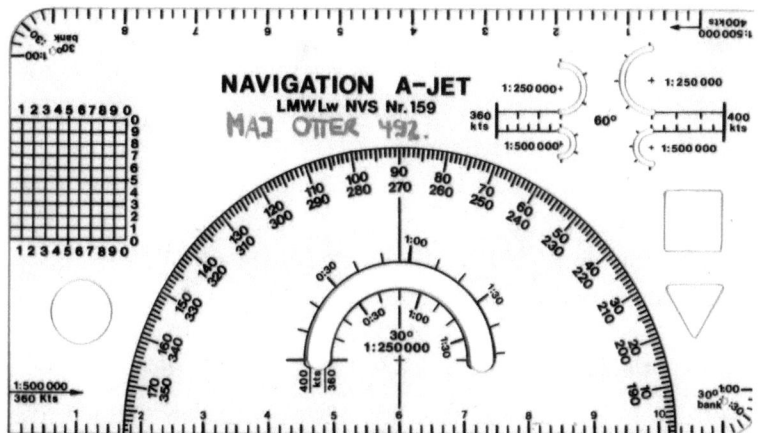

Navigation template for the Alpha Jet. Using this template, we planned low-level routes on 1:250,000 scale flight maps.

The physical and psychological strain on pilots flying at low altitudes was significant. For young aviators without years of low-level experience, the stress was comparable to driving at high speed on a three-lane highway with narrow lanes, overtaking massive trucks while nervously maintaining a safe distance.

With years of routine, a pilot would gradually lower his personal "altitude barrier" and grow accustomed to the low heights and high speeds.

In the G.91, the altimeter was unreliable at low altitudes, whereas the radar altimeter in the Alpha Jet was accurate. I recall a low-level mission over the Baltic Sea in the G.91. Our standard low-level altitude over water was 250 feet. I reduced my altitude further and briefly flew at an estimated 50 feet - about 15 meters above the water - at 360 knots. Due to the so-called "ground effect," the cushion of air beneath the aircraft, my altimeter read "-100 feet," indicating I was flying below the water's surface. The altimeter only became somewhat reliable above 250 feet.

Pilots who descended below their psychological "altitude barrier" often experienced a decline in navigational accuracy. Tests showed that experienced pilots rarely dropped below their personal minimum altitude, yet still navigated with precision. Younger pilots, on the other hand, forced themselves to fly as low as possible, focusing on low-altitude flying rather than navigation, which led to course deviations.

Even seasoned pilots, after extended periods of extreme low-level flying, tended to climb slightly higher due to increasing psychological stress. This primarily concerned altitudes below 250 feet, approximately 75 meters above ground level.

Back to Maps, Compass, and Clock.

During simulated combat missions, pilots had to perform numerous tasks. Courses and flight times in minutes and seconds were marked on the map for quick reference. Restricted areas, obstacles like radio masts and towers, the forward line of own troops (FLOT), and more were also noted.

In addition to navigation, the pilot had to maintain formation position, operate weapon systems, communicate via radio, adjust the Identification Friend or Foe (IFF) codes regularly, monitor the airspace, watch for enemy threats, and, if necessary, execute defensive maneuvers to prevent being shot down or endangering the formation. These tasks significantly impacted navigation and formation flying.

The highest priority was completing the assigned mission - attacking a designated target - on which the lives of ground troops might depend. Success was mandatory, no matter the challenges.

In peacetime operations, flight noise over critical areas, large towns, or cities was to be minimized whenever possible. At 400 knots (766 km/h), the G.91 and Alpha Jet's speed during attack phases, turn radii spanned several kilometers. These turn radii influenced navigation, particularly regarding restricted zones, no-fly areas, and noise abatement.

Wind had some impact on flight paths during low-level navigation but became significant only over several minutes. For short segments of one, two, or three minutes, wind influence could be ignored.

Since wind drift could not be calculated mid-flight - it constantly changed direction and strength over hundreds of kilometers - pilots had to estimate its impact and adjust by feel and experience based on observed drift.

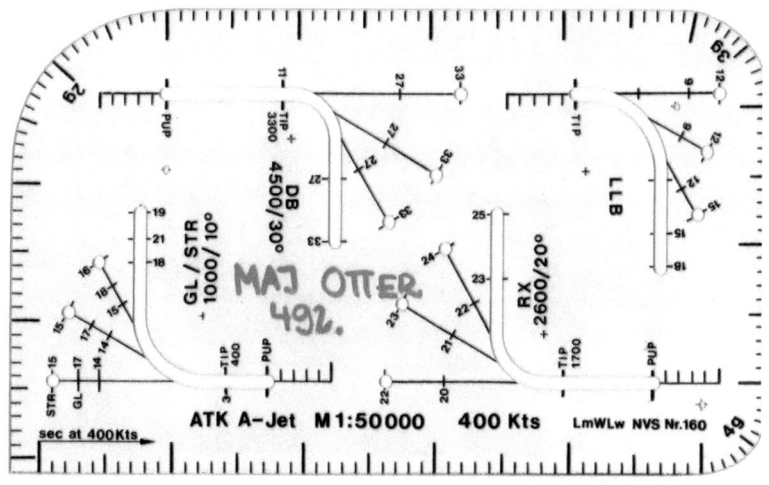

Navigation template at 1:50,000 scale for the attack phase

Fighter-bomber pilots were expected to reach their assigned target at the exact attack time. NATO allowed a tolerance of +/- 30 seconds, but internally, the standard was +/- 10 seconds.

Two to three minutes before the planned target time, pilots reached the Initial Point (IP), which they had to cross at the calculated time, exact speed of 400 knots, and predetermined heading toward the target. Navigation from the IP to the target was conducted using a 1:50,000 scale map to identify every forest edge, clearing, and path.

To locate and attack a concealed and camouflaged tank, pilots had only a few seconds to identify the target. Without a large-scale map, this would have been impossible.

Planning the attack phase required a specialized template that accounted for turn radii. Missing the target by just 50 meters could mean failing the mission and endangering the pilot and the formation.

Unlike the F-104G "Starfighter"and F-4F "Phantom" squadrons, we didn't have centralized flight planning offices staffed by specialists who prepared or significantly assisted with flight plans. Precision low-level navigation was the result of extensive individual preparation by the pilots in the formation.

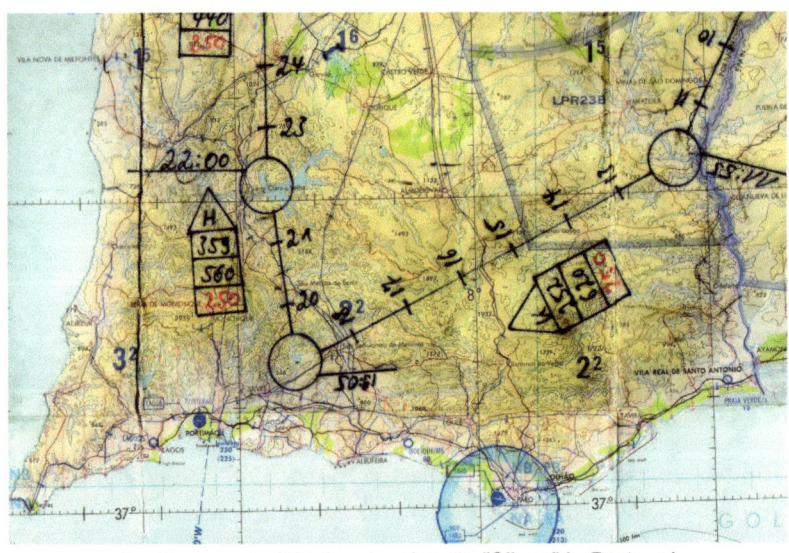

Southern part of the low-level route "Silves" in Portugal.

In flight, success depended entirely on the lead pilot, who, alone in their single-seater aircraft, managed all tasks without technical assistance.

Near miss with a Starfighter

Throttle full forward, the Orpheus engine roared. The brakes on the G.91 were underpowered and couldn't typically hold against maximum static thrust, causing the aircraft to creep forward, centimeter by centimeter. My eyes scanned the instruments one last time, from left to right across the cockpit. The engine gauges on the front-right panel all showed values in the "green zone."

G.91 R3 FBW 49 taxing

Releasing the brakes, I corrected the alignment on the runway with small braking adjustments as the Gina accelerated down the strip. The G.91 lacked nose wheel steering, so steering on the ground was done entirely with the brakes. After approximately 21 seconds, I reached 125 knots. At 145 knots, I rotated and lifted off.

The aircraft was "cleaned up" immediately - gear and flaps retracted - and, with all instruments still in the green, the plane accelerated to 360 knots, our low-level cruise speed. The sky was clear, with visibility limited only by the horizon. The "Autobahn" disappeared beneath me, entering the forest near Odelzhausen in my 12 o'clock position.

This point marked the NZP, or "Navigational Zero Point", the starting location for our low-level routes.

I reseted the stopwatch to "0," retrieved the low-level map from beneath my left thigh, read the first course heading - 271 degrees - and scanned the airspace for other aircraft. At the departure and approach points of airfields, collision risks with other aircraft were significantly higher. Flying precisely over the intersection of the Autobahn and the forest edge, I started the stopwatch and checked the course on the compass. The G.91 flew steadily over the flat terrain.

Mission Objective: Simulated bombing a bridge in the Black Forest.

My task was to simulate an attack on a railway bridge in the Black Forest, carrying two 250 kg bombs, also simulated for this flight.

As the terrain became more rugged during the low-level flight, the ride became bumpier. On a hot day, the jolting was reminiscent of driving over old cobblestone streets at 75 miles/h.

At each waypoint, the same checks had to be completed:

- Check time.
- Set new course.
- Verify engine instruments.
- Check remaining fuel against the flight calculations.
- Scan the airspace for other aircraft.

Five minutes remained until the Initial Point (IP). From this waypoint, the attack phase would begin:

- Throttle to 95% power to accelerate to 400 knots.

- Set weapon switch to bombs.
- Stow the low-level map under the left thigh.
- Retrieve the 1:50,000 target map from under the right thigh.
- Reset the stopwatch to 0.
- Throttle back to 92% to hold exactly 400 knots.
- Input calculated values for a dive attack into the gun sight.
- Make the final course correction to align with the attack
  heading.
- Start the stopwatch - time was running!

The IP was typically no more than three minutes from the target:

- Correct course to the left.
- Throttle to 95% to accelerate from 390 to 400 knots.
- Scan the airspace for other aircraft.
- Activate the main weapons switch.
- Correct course to the right.
- At 142 seconds, pull the stick back.

During one of my final flights in the G.91, 1979

- At 152 seconds, roll the aircraft inverted to achieve a dive angle of -10°.
  - Visually acquire the target.
- Make course corrections.
- Check altitude to reach the planned release height.
- Adjust the target in the sight.
- Press the release button - the target camera began recording for post-mission analysis.
- Pull the stick back to recover the aircraft.
- Check the clock and note the exact time over the target for later documentation.
- Turn onto the egress course.
- Press the stopwatch again.
- Switch the weapon controls to "OFF".
- Stow the target map under the right thigh.
- Retrieve the low-level map from under the left thigh.
- Throttle back to 360 knots.
- Visually acquire the first waypoint after the target.
- Reset the stopwatch to "0".
- Read the next course from the map.
- Fly precisely over the navigation point.
- Start the stopwatch.
- Adjust speed.
- Throttle to 89%.
- Check the time.
- Correct the course.
- Verify all engine instruments are in the green zone.
- Ensure fuel is sufficient.

The return flight from a simulated attack had begun.

An Unexpected Encounter

This detailed account illustrates the tasks during a tactical attack on a ground target. Should a pilot face enemy fire, additional mental tasks would come into play. The time span of the attack described here ranged between two and five minutes.

Suddenly, out of the corner of my eye, I noticed a movement for a split second - a moment later, an F-104G flashed over my cockpit, coming from the 11 o'clock position. Hidden by the cockpit strut, I hadn't seen the "104" in time. We passed each other at a combined speed of 810 knots, approximately 1,500 km/h, equivalent to around 420 meters per second. We were no more than 30 feet apart. I instinctively yanked the stick to the right, far too late and to slow to prevent a collision had it been necessary.

We were both lucky. Luck was essential to make it to retirement in this profession.

The Mission resumes...
- Correct course.
- Check time.
- Scan the airspace for another aircraft. (Low-level flights were mostly conducted in formations.)
- Switch radio frequency.

Shortly afterward, my low-level map began to tremble - the adrenaline was still pumping. Unable to steady my hand, I rested it on my thigh. A minute later, everything was back to normal. The low-level map lay steady in my hand once more:

- Correct course.
- Check time.
- Verify engine instruments are in the green.
- Ensure fuel is sufficient.

After 55 minutes, I landed back at Fürsty.
Mission accomplished.

Cross-Country

Cross-country flights, known in aviation slang as "Cross Countries" (XC), had been popular missions since our training days at Sheppard AFB. My XCs at Sheppard AFB were flown in the T-37 to Denver, Colorado, and El Paso, Texas, and in the T-38 to England AFB in Louisiana, Homestead in Florida, and Reese AFB in Texas.

My first cross-country flight in the Fiat G.91 "Gina" took us to Valencia, Spain. Not that I had any say in where we were going - no, my flight instructor, an "old" Captain, wanted to stock up his home bar with Spanish brandy. Cross-country flights were generally conducted in a formation of two aircraft for safety reasons. Accompanying us were my crewmate and his flight instructor, also an "old" Captain.

We took off in July 1977 from "Fürsty" in formation flight. The route led us over Colmar, Lyon, Lourdes, with a stopover in Istres, France, and then to Valencia, Spain.

My flight instructor had flown to Spain many times before (to restock his bar) and was well aware of the poor radio communications. The signal quality was abysmal, and the English proficiency of spanish air traffic controllers at the time was atrocious.

On the way to Valencia, we were "Number 2" in the formation, so I didn't have to handle the radio communication myself - I just listened in and confirmed instructions when needed. My task was to operate our radio whenever a new frequency was assigned.

GAF 3155 lead aircraft contacted Barcelona Control:
"Barcelona control, this is German Air Force 3155,"
"Barcelona control, this is German Air Force 3155,"
"Barcelona control, this is German Air Force 3155,"
(Repeated several times.)

"Hey, Fritze, can you hear anything?" my flight instructor was asked from the lead aircraft IP.

"Nope, that's normal," he replied.

"Hey, Fritze, can you make the call?"

"Yes, I'm calling now," my instructor replied.

"Barcelona control, this is German Air Force 3155."

Finally, a response:

"Gerrmann Air Force 3 1 5 5, thiss is Barzelona Controll, Bon dia."

My flight instructor reported our position:

"Barcelona control, German Air Force 3155 is inbound Valencia."

Then, in a distinctive English-Spanish accent, the lead flight instructor's voice came over the radio:

"Gerrmann Air Force... cleared to Valencia... des-cend to one-zerro-zerro... go Valencia Towwerr, tree fourr one pointt sevven."

Fifty miles later, we contacted Valencia Tower and landed safely.

After landing, one "old" Captain asked the other:

"Hey, Fritze, how did you manage that? I've been flying to Spain

Approach of or G.91 T3 with Instructor Pilot (1977)

for ten years, and "Barcelona Control' has never responded to me. I always thought Barcelona Radar was out of our radio range."

To which my flight instructor replied:

"You've got to know how to make the call!"

In truth, we never actually established radio contact with Barcelona Control. The other flight instructor pranked my flight instructor in the air by imitating Barcelona Control.

Instructor Pilot's mishap

It was a sunny day in Bavaria, with a postcard-blue, cloudless sky over "Fürsty." If I could have chosen any training mission, I would have opted for a low-level navigation flight, targeting a practice site near the Danube, and returning to "Fürsty" along the Alps, taking a glimpse at the Andechs Monastery on the way back.

Looking at the mission board, I saw that I was assigned to fly an "Out and Back" with a student, planned from "Fürsty" (EDSF) to land in Husum (EDNH) and return two hours later.

My student was a WSO (Weapons Systems Officer) preparing for the Tornado conversion course in Cottesmore, UK. As far as I recall, he was part of the last WSO training course we conducted with the Fiat G.91 T3. I was one of the youngest Instructor Pilots in "Fürsty," among the final four IPs, being retrained on the new Alpha Jet.

"Seniority before youth?"

No - it was simply a matter of the remaining service time in the Air Force of the pilots.

Preparation for the Flight.

The flight to Husum was planned by my student, he registered with flight operations, and briefed by him during our preflight briefing. As an instructor pilot, my role was to oversee all preparations and provide support or corrections only when necessary.

Our flight was planned as a high-altitude route under IFR (Instrument Flight Rules), despite the clear skies over Bavaria.

After takeoff, we were to follow departure route SF1, leading to Giebelstadt (GBL CH47). From there, we would fly to Frankfurt (FFM CH89), follow airway TB1 to Osnabrück (OSB CH20), then to Nordholz (NDO CH118), and finally direct to Husum. The approach was planned as a Hi-TACAN instrument approach to runway 03. If traffic and fuel allowed, we would perform a GCA (Ground Controlled Approach) guided by Husum's Radar as a secondary instrument approach, followed by a landing.

The two-hour layover in Husum would give us enough time to greet former squadron mates, enjoy a coffee, and hopefully have a shrimp sandwich for lunch. Guest pilots were always provided with meals in the squadron's kitchen. My student was responsible for the flight plan and weather briefing for the return flight, while I supervised and supported him as needed.

The preflight briefing was conducted confidently by my student. Before leaving the bunker we briefly checked the weather monitor together and then headed to our aircraft on the large tarmac.

The Flight to Husum.

After completing the preflight inspection, starting the engine, taxiing to the runway, and taking off, we were en route to Husum.

As planned, my WSO student guided me through the departure procedure, calling out headings and altitudes to follow. He handled radio communications with the ground stations, changed frequencies as instructed, and adjusted the channels on the TACAN navigation system.

At 31,000 feet, I enjoyed the view from our cruising altitude, occasionally scanning the instruments. Everything seemed to indicate a calm, a problem-free training flight.

Over Frankfurt, "Rhein-Radar" cleared us for a direct route to Husum:

"Fortuna, you are cleared direct Husum, heading is 005."

"Roger, Fortuna direct Husum," my backseater replied.

My WSO student implemented the instruction, switched to the TACAN channel for Husum (CH85), and instructed me to set a heading of 005. Flying at 31,000 feet, Mach 0.80, we continued northward toward Schleswig-Holstein.

A Suspicious Silence.

After some time, my student noted:

"Captain, I'm not getting a TACAN distance reading."

"No problem," I replied.

"We're still outside the TACAN range for Husum. The distance indicator will come awake eventually."

We continued flying north. Thin cirrus clouds began appearing at our altitude, gradually thickening over the next 20 minutes.

"How many miles is it from Frankfurt to Husum?" I asked my backseater.

"201 miles, Captain," he replied.

The clear blue sky turned gray, and the view of the ground disappeared behind an increasingly dark veil. My focus shifted from the landscape to the instruments.

A Subtle Mistake.

A couple of minutes later, the TACAN instrument displayed a distance of 179 miles. We passed Osnabrück and Nordholz, still on a direct course to Husum. Everything looked good: instruments, radio contact, and navigation indicators. My student had everything under control.

At some point, "Rhein-Radar" handed us off to "Lippe Radar," and then to "Eider Control." I reminded my student to inform "Eider Control" of our planned TACAN approach to Husum, which he did promptly and correctly.

"You are cleared to FL20, HI-TACAN approach into Husum runway 03. Report leaving Initial Approach Fix," came the clearance from "Eider Control."

We were now flying in dense clouds, with the cloud base forecasted to be sufficient for our landing. Our alternate airfield was "Leck" (EDNL), with other options at Eggebeck and Jagel.

Descending to FL20 (20,000 feet) for the approach, my student gave accurate instructions. I followed his directions, monitored the approach procedure, and referred to the approach book on my left kneeboard. Everything matched up.

At FL20, flying at 280 knots, precisely on the radial for Husum's approach procedure, my backseater reported:

"Fortuna initial approach fix, leaving FL20."

I pitched the nose 10 degrees down, reduced engine power to 80%, and followed his course and altitude instructions. Then, a question from "Eider Control":

"Fortuna, are you sure your destination is Husum?"

"Fortuna, that's correct," I confirmed. My student, whose task was to handle communications, was too stunned to respond.

"Fortuna, you are overhead Leck airfield!" the controller informed us.

I quickly suspected a possible error.

"Did you set the TACAN Channel for Husum?" I asked my student.

"Yes, I did," he replied. "What channel did you tune? Channel 85?"

"No, channel 28," he answered.

"Oh, shit. Husum is CH85. Leck is CH28", he realized.

I took over radio communications and requested a handoff to GCA for a radar-guided approach to Husum. From this approach, we safely landed on runway 03.

How did this error happen? We had flown the approach procedure for Husum using Leck's TACAN station in dense clouds.

On my student's mission sheet, the "Landing" line was correctly filled out with Husum (EDNH) CH85. The next line, for the "Alternate" (diversion airfield), listed Leck, CH28. He had misread the line when setting the TACAN channel.

Because we were initially flying without TACAN distance readings, and we saw no significant deviation when the first distance appeared, we both assumed the indication was correct.

A "recheck" was not performed. I didn't question the values either.

But Leck is directly behind Husum from Frankfurt, and the distances are nearly identical when flying approximate headings.

Once again, we were lucky. This experience reinforced an essential lesson: Mistakes can happen, even when everything seems to be running smoothly.

Google Maps.

Capo Frasca

A Sunny Day in Sardinia: Life in Cagliari and Decimomannu

The scent of "dolci" (cakes and pastries) and espresso filled the air. Beautiful, flirtatious "ragazze", walking arm-in-arm in groups of four or five - rarely in pairs, never alone - passed by, giggling and casting coy glances, but they always seemed "out of reach." Honking cars, policewomen twirling their batons to direct traffic, and the sense, that even without them, the chaos of cars and scooters would move at the same disorganized rhythm.

Stylish women admired the displays in the expensive boutique windows. Familiar faces of German soldiers strolled by or relaxed in Street-Cafés, enjoying their evenings. This was Cagliari in the 1970s, the capital of Sardinia.

Morning Routine at "Casa Trintasette"

At just before seven in the morning, we left "Casa Trintasette" - our accommodation building No. 37 - on foot, heading to the mess hall. Breakfast in the noisy dining room, which reminded us of a Mexican "Cantina", consisted of clattering tin dishes and tasteless coffee.

A resident Instructor Pilot, a "permanent" stationed at the base, had advised us to drink mineral water with a pinch of salt during breakfast to counteract the day's salt loss. After breakfast, we typically hitchhiked to the squadron building and operations center; otherwise, it was a 20-minute walk.

Following the "Morning Briefing," we gathered for the "Mission Briefing" led by the flight leader. That day, I was assigned as "Gunsmoke 2" in a four-ship mission heading to the Capo Frasca Firing-Range.

Preparing for Takeoff

At 10:30 AM, I climbed into the cockpit, already sweating as the thermometer read 31°C (88°F) in the shadow. Beads of sweat ran down my forehead and into my eyes. Surrounding me, the deafening roar of engines screamed and whistled, a cacophony I often experienced on Decimomannu's tarmac, surrounded by aircraft of various types.

As the second aircraft, I released my brakes and followed my flight leader cautiously, higher temperatures demanded more power to get the aircraft moving. We taxied along the taxiway to the far end of the airfield, stopping near the runway threshold in front of the arming wall.

My position was to the left of the flight leader, with "Gunsmoke Three" on my left and "Gunsmoke Four" next to him. We placed our hands visibly on the dashboard or dangled them out of the cockpit if the canopy was open while the ground crew removed safety pins from the weapon stations. This visible gesture ensured no accidental engagement of weapon switches. The ground crew held up the pins, marked with the bright red "REMOVE BEFORE FLIGHT" flags, for the pilots to confirm, before stowing them. These flags, incidentally, were highly sought-after souvenirs.

Takeoff and Flight to Capo Frasca

"Gunsmoke flight, channel 14, go."

The flight leader taxied ahead, and I followed, setting channel 14, the local tower frequency.

"Gunsmoke flight, check in."

"Two," ... "Three," ... "Four."

"Gunsmoke flight cleared for takeoff runway 35R. Cleared to cross."

"Gunsmoke flight cleared takeoff."

The flight leader released his brakes, and each aircraft followed at eight-second intervals.

We executed a "High-Low-High" takeoff. The leader climbed steeply right after liftoff, just ten knots above stall speed. I deliberately stayed low to avoid his jet wash. Despite this, I briefly entered his turbulence, which violently rocked my aircraft and pushed it into a right turn. I quickly corrected but was momentarily shaken, there was no time to dwell on it.

"Four airborne."

The call reported to the flight-leader that all members of the formation were in the air and would catch up to assume the planned positions.

We flew over scorched meadows, rocky fields, and typical southern villages toward the Gulf of Oristano. Our destination was Capo Frasca, an Italian air-to-ground gunnery range.

The Gunnery Mission

We checked in on the range frequency and heard a four-ship of F-104G's sign off after completing their firing-training, heading back to "Decimo," the nickname for Decimomannu.

In an "Echelon Right" formation, we passed over the gunnery range. Above the gunnery flag for the cannon exercise, the flight lead made a left turn into the pattern.

Weapons switch to "Gun",

Guns set to High,

I prepared for high firing rates.

The flight leader, already in a left turn with a 10° dive toward the target flag, called:

"Lead in hot."

The range officer responded:

"Lead cleared hot."

I watched smoke trailing from the lead aircraft's cannon and noted, "Ah, that's what it looks like."

As my turn approached, I called:

"Two in hot."

Switching the "Weapon Hot" safety directly in front of me, I received the response:

"Two cleared hot."

For the first time, I was cleared to fire the G.91's 30mm cannons.

My gun sight's aiming point, the "Pipper," wasn't aligned with the target. Adjusting, I saw it veer left. Using the rudder pedals, I overcorrected, pushing the Pipper to the right. The ground loomed close, and my mind raced. Acting on instinct, I fired as the Pipper approached the target.

"Drdrdrdrdrdrdrdrdrdr!"

The cannons roared, rattling the aircraft. Startled, I pulled the stick abruptly back to recover. In the next moment, I processed the experience while rejoining the pattern.

The G-meter read 6.5g - well above the usual 4g. Inside the sweltering cockpit, at nearly 50°C (122°F), my heart raced between 160 and 180 bpm.

Fiat G.91 T3 with training bomb rack

After three cannon passes, we proceeded to fire rockets and drop four bombs, the last two in a "skip bombing" exercise from just 50 feet (15 meters) at 400 knots. The target was the "Skip Garden," a simulated target for napalm bombing.

We returned to Decimomannu in a four-ship formation. The Fiat G.91 T3 (Trainer) was not equipped with cannons, so pilots experienced their first live fire in the single-seat variant, a memorable and nerve-wracking event for all.

I wasn't the only student who over-pulled the aircraft during my first live-fire mission. Some exceeded 7g, requiring up to three days of inspection for potential overloading.

Two to three live-fire missions per day were standard in Decimomannu.

After the day's flights, we returned to "Casa Trintasette" for a much-needed shower, only to find the water had run dry. In the late 1970s, this was "standard procedure" in Decimomannu.

Even visits to the restroom required caution: one pull of the chain would empty the tank, and no water would refill. Truly, "Italian standard in the 70s."

Evenings often ended at "Joseph's", a snack-bar near the main gate where a glass of "vino rosso" were 500 Lire. Afterward, we'd take the bus to Cagliari, reliving the same impressions as in the beginning:

"The scent of fresh 'dolci' and espresso, beautiful girls, and so on…"

At "Joseph's" across from the main gate of the "Aeroporto di Decimomannu," we had our last nightcap after the usual return from Cagliari.

Recce-Flight

In 1977, during our retraining and "Europeanization" phase - an adaptation period to learn to fly under European flight rules, with European weather conditions, airspace structures, tactical procedures, low-level flight, and many other aspects that differed significantly from training operations in the U.S. We also trained in tactical aerial reconnaissance.

The Fiat G.91 was equipped with three built-in Vinten F95 MK3 cameras: one forward-facing and two angled to each side. Solo flight assignments occasionally included the task of bringing back

a target photo, which served as proof that we had successfully located our objective during the solo mission. Naturally, the cameras could also be used to photograph each other in flight, resulting in some impressive and now nostalgic images of the Fiat G.91 in action.

During the summer, nude bathing in secluded spots along riverbanks was already popular. Among some of the younger pilots, word quickly spread about a bathing spot along the "Isar" River south of Munich, where, on sunny days, nudists could always be found.

For certain pilots, it became an enticing idea to make a brief pass over the "Isarauen" - also known as "Pupplinger Au" - after a

Recce with the forward camera of the G.91 low level flight (1977).

low-level mission, provided their fuel reserves allowed. Stretching several kilometers, the Isar offered an ideal reconnaissance target for a "River Recce" mission, where hidden bathing coves could reveal "opportunity targets". Among specific pilots, the "reconnaissance results" and "precise geographical coordinates" of such spots were shared discreetly and in confidence.

Unfortunately, I only learned about this many years later.

The photographic results using the film material were excellent.

Survival Training

Squadron Alert at 04:30 a.m.

Three pilots from our planned mission were already in the briefing room preparing for the operation. We noted down the assigned aircraft, their locations in the shelters, and recorded all the necessary data on our knee-boards. This included the planned TOT (Time Over Target), altitudes, code words, encryption tables, call signs, frequencies, and rendezvous points, essential in case a pilot had to temporarily leave the formation due to clouds or an attack by enemy aircraft.

We received a final weather update and gathered all the documents we would need during the flight. Each of us folded our low-level maps (folding techniques were highly personal), which we had prepared in advance with all essential information about the route and the target. The intelligence officer provided detailed information on enemy air defenses and photos of the target.

We then convened at a table to review the mission plan in detail. Focus was heightened since the operation involved live weapons. Afterward, we performed a final review with the operations officer.

A Sergeant had prepared our flight helmets and life vests equipped with emergency radios. We carried personal weapons, a Walther PPK in 7.65mm caliber, in shoulder holsters beneath our leather jackets. Our squadron patches were removed from our flight suits, and no personal items were permitted during such realistic missions. Personal IDs, wallets, and family photos were left at the squadron; any such items

Walther PPK 7.65mm

113

could be used against us in captivity.

Our driver, Karl, waited outside the bunker in a VW van to transport us to the shelters where our armed aircraft was ready.

I placed my helmet on the cockpit edge and stored my documents and flight maps between the dashboard and the windscreen. Together with the ground crew, I conducted the exterior check of the aircraft and its weapon load.

Our target was the air-to-ground gunnery range in "Putlos", just 10 minutes (about 60 miles) from the real targets in East Germany that we would have attacked in a defensive war. These contingency plans were already prepared and stored in files.

If we were shot down or captured as prisoners of war, we relied on the training from three survival courses. If our aircraft was critically damaged, we were trained to eject over open water whenever possible to increase the chances of survival. Ejecting over land would almost certainly lead to capture.

Survival Training: Water and Land

After completing flight training at Sheppard AFB, we attended the "Water Survival Training Course SV86A" in Homestead, Florida.

The first two days covered classroom instruction on the survival gear included in every ejection seat: Handling the life raft, flare gun, fishing hooks and line, emergency rations, drinking water, night lights, signal mirrors, and whistles.

Training tower at Homestead AFB.

Practical exercises began with drills at a training tower, simulating every step from ejection to water entry. The site overlooked the Turtle Beach nuclear power plant, and the water was pleasantly warm, likely warmed by reactor cooling water.

Next came exercises in Biscayne Bay. Suspended by a parachute harness over the water from a converted landing craft, we were dropped into the sea. A motorboat then towed us through the water as we practiced flipping onto our backs, spreading our legs for stability, and keeping our faces above water.

At a given signal, we unfastened the harness, simulating a parachute water landing. Now on our own, we used our survival kits, especially the dinghy. Entering the dinghy required a specific technique: pulling it under your torso and sliding in belly-first to conserve energy. Extreme care was needed to avoid puncturing the raft with equipment. While patch kits were included, prevention was better than repair.

Once I was stable in the raft, my legs dangled in the warm water. We wore standard flight suits but swapped leather boots for sneakers, covered with black socks. This precaution was due to a "shark warning" that day, the socks were meant to avoid attracting sharks to bright sneakers.

On July 28, 1976, a scorching day, the saltwater left a crust on our faces. Without freshwater, our only relief was briefly splashing our faces with saltwater, which burned the sunburned skin.

Encounter with "Sharks"

One hundred feet away, an FBI training participant in his dinghy yelled at me:

"Have you seen sharks?"

"No, I haven't seen any," I replied.

"But have you seen the shadows in the water? They may be sharks!" he exclaimed. He added in a frightened voice, "I think they're bumping my raft!"

Later at the officers' mess, he admitted he was too scared to dip his feet into the water or even touch it with his hands. The "bumps" he felt, however, were stabilizing water pockets attached to the raft. These occasionally knocked against the raft bottom in rough waters - not sharks!

After hours at the sea, a helicopter arrived to rescue us. Each participant had to follow precise procedures to avoid static discharge from the winch. The rescue strap was placed under the armpits, and arms were crossed over the abdomen to ensure a secure lift into the helicopter.

When five "shipwrecked" individuals had been rescued, the helicopter flew them back to the shore to retrieve the next participants from the water. The rest of the training followed standard military routine.

Jet pilots are self-confident. I already wrote about this in the chapter "Fighter Pilots." This self-confidence is not just about the ability to fly a modern fighter plane or to precisely place a bomb on a target. A "Fighter Pilot" needs this self-assurance in one-on-one air combat or when landing an aircraft safely under the most adverse weather conditions.

But what kind of confidence does a pilot need when his aircraft is no longer airworthy, when the technology fails, and he has to make an emergency landing in inhospitable terrain, in polar regions, or in a steppe where food and water are scarce? What if an enemy shoots down his aircraft, whether in an air-to-air engagement or with a surface-to-air missile, over hostile territory? If he lands behind enemy lines by parachute or has to make an emergency landing with his helicopter, trying to evade capture but ultimately finding himself as a prisoner of war in the hands of his adversary? What if he expects that an enemy will treat prisoners inhumanely, torture them, and not adhere to the laws of war? If one has the confidence to fly combat missions under such conditions, then one must also have the confidence to master such situations as best as possible.

"Four men left door - four men right door" - every pilot who participated in survival training in "Schongau" knew these calls. They were the instructions for four soldiers to climb to the top platform of the jump tower at the Airborne and Air Transport School in Altenstadt and jump down from a height of 45 feet while harnessed. It was an exercise in overcoming one's inner resistance and practicing parachute procedures.

The "Survival Training for Flight Personnel" is now called "SERE" - Survival, Evasion, Resistance, and Escape. We used to call it "Survival Behavior, Capture, Prisoner of War, and Escape." The course was an integral part of the general pilot training.

During training, we learned about the survival equipment carried in ejection seats as the "survival pack." Other than our personal weapon and ammunition, we had no additional gear. The academic lessons focused on topics that could not be practiced, such as injuries and medical self-care, capture, captivity, and the psychological and physical aspects of torture.

However, the practical training dominated the 14-day training. We learned how to handle a parachute, shoot with foreign or captured weapons in enemy territory, build a shelter using a parachute, start a fire in the rain, and communicate with searching aircraft using a signal mirror. We also learned what food sources were available in the wilderness, how to find drinking water, and how to collect nighttime dew for hydration.

Those who had been Boy Scouts as teenagers had an undeniable advantage. Some of their knowledge was refreshed, such as determining directions using tree growth patterns or finding the North Star to navigate. We learned how to move and orient ourselves in rough terrain, how to cross obstacles and rivers, and how to stay alert for threatening sounds.

This was no camping trip, the instructors of the VI. Company pushed us to our limits. Under pouring rain, the training frayed our nerves after only a few hours.

During the practical training in the "Sauwald" region, north of Bavaria's "Forggensee" and not far from the famous church "Wieskirche", we were given only minimal rations. These were supplemented by whatever food we could find in the wilderness or steal while "breaking through" enemy lines. Fish could be caught, and live chickens would be stolen. Few of our participants had ever caught a fish or killed

Each participant slaughtered a chicken for himself.

and gutted a chicken before, preparing it over an open fire. Even these extra rations did not fully satisfy our stomach.

And we were exhausted. Each night, we only got a few hours of sleep. We moved continuously, either in small groups or alone. We were given only a small section of a map and had to reach predesignated contact points. There, at an agreed-upon time, an escape helper would meet us.

During the Cold War, such "escape networks" existed in potential deployment areas east of the "Oder" River. Infantry troops were deployed to track us down and capture us. Those who were caught[10] could expect harsh treatment. Hunger, sleep deprivation, and what felt like psychological torture pushed us to our limits. Repeated interrogations stretched us to the edge of our endurance.

There were, however, boundaries. No one wanted to ruin the health or career of a pilot in whom millions of Deutsche Marks had been invested in training.

The learning outcome of this training depended on one's personal mindset, the ability to overcome one's inner resistance, push one's physical and psychological limits, and learn behavioral techniques to resist harsh treatment and torture in captivity. It was essential to endure such situations for a period and to recognize the moment when giving in was necessary.

During the Cold War, we trained for the "worst case" scenario. When we remember the execution of prisoners and hostages by the so-called Islamic State in Syria, it is clear that even in the future, fighter pilots must engage with these realities and prepare themselves through rigorous training.

At the "Sea Survival" training with Naval Air Squadron 3 in "Nordholz", we repeated the fundamental lessons of our training in Homestead, Florida, adapting them to the climatic conditions of Europe.

---

[10]   Escape from Laos – by Dieter Dengler

During my first sea-survival-training in Germany, the water temperature was 6°C. In Florida, we only wore our flight suits in the water, but in the North Sea, we had to wear a cold-water survival suit to stay alive. Pilots called this suit the "Frankenstein" and wore it on all low-level flights over the North- and Baltic Sea, summer and winter alike.

The "Open Sea" training in Nordholz completed the American survival training and had to be repeated every three years. Training in the North Sea was only suspended when water temperatures dropped below 2°C.

With thorough survival training in all aspects, pilots were able to carry out their missions with confidence.

**You Train as You Fight,
and You Fight as You Train.**

Sea survival training in the cold "North Sea".

Sea survival in the North Sea.

The effect of the down wash of the rescue-helicopter.

Möns Klint

Captain Wille's Motto: "No One Flies Lower Than Me!"

Captain Wille ended his preflight briefing, as he often did, with the statement: "No one flies lower than me!"

We were flying a "Baltic Low Level" mission, a low-level flight over the Baltic Sea along the five-mile zone near the former East German border. This was my first mission over the Baltic in a four-ship formation. Previously, I had only trained for low-level flights in two-ship formations as part of the squadron orientation program.

We departed the Husum control zone heading south, then turned east, flew over Kiel Bay, and reported "Feet Wet", indicating that we were no longer flying over land.

Over the Baltic Sea, we began our descent to 250 feet, our low-level altitude. As "Osprey 2," I held my position 6,000 feet (one mile) to the left or right of my flight leader, depending on the situation, in the "Fluid Four" formation. The second section, "Osprey 3" and "Osprey 4," followed in the same formation one mile behind us.

The Challenge of Low-level flight over the sea

Flying low over the sea was a unique challenge. There was almost no radio communication; our focus was entirely on the formation, our aircraft, and the demands of low-level navigation. Navigation relied solely on "time and heading", with speed and wind drift corrected based on real-time observations since wind forecasts were often inaccurate.

The feeling of flying very low, free from obstacles, was indescribable. As a wingman, I didn't need to constantly check the altimeter; I used my flight leader as my altitude reference. By keeping my aircraft at the same relative position on the horizon as his, I automatically maintained the minimum altitude. However, if my leader dipped below the minimum altitude, so did I, often without realizing it at first.

This was particularly dangerous in smooth water and hazy visibility, where judging altitude became nearly impossible.

Captain Wille's mantra echoed in my head: "No one flies lower than me!"

I carefully kept Wille's aircraft in sight on the horizon. Occasionally, the masts of passing sailboats seemed to grow taller, but I followed the instruction to keep my leading aircraft at the horizon.

At the easternmost waypoint of our low-level route, we executed a 180° turn to head west, roughly toward the mainland. I was fully focused, with no time to glance at the instruments. My eyes were locked onto the flight leader, ensuring I didn't fly lower than him and maintained proper position.

Radio silence was broken: "Osprey flight - line abreast, go!"

I had been briefed by squadron mates on how to execute this maneuver. All four aircraft adjusted to fly in a side-by-side "line abreast" formation.

Captain Wille repeated: "No one flies lower than me!"

The spray from the waves was minimal, with swells no higher

The cliffs of Møns Klint. Photo by Christiane Appel.

than one meter. My focus was on Wille, who was to my left. I needed to keep him in my 9 o'clock position, over my left shoulder, to maintain alignment.

Approaching the Cliffs of Møns Klint

The bright white cliffs loomed ahead, towering like a vertical wall. Tension rose; I knew what was coming up.

I alternated my gaze between Wille to my left and the cliffs ahead, my head swiveling every half-second. Left, forward, left, forward - 20, 30 times, I lost count. There was no time to glance right at my fellow wingmen. I knew "Osprey 3" and "Osprey 4" were as focused as I was, with "Osprey 4" following "Osprey 3" in the same way I followed Wille.

The cliffs grew brighter and taller, rising above the horizon.

"No one flies lower than me!"

The dark shadows of the cliff folds became visible. The cliffs now stretched beyond my cockpit's field of view, and I tried to increase the speed of my glances between Wille and the cliffs.

Finally, I pulled the stick back hard, yanking it into my chest to avoid smashing into the towering white cliffs. The cliffs passed swiftly beneath my cockpit, vanishing behind me as I rolled my aircraft inverted to break the climb. I leveled out and searched for my flight leader, spotting him below me to my left.

Easing the stick forward, I descended until I had "Osprey Lead" back on the horizon.

After all, "No one flies lower than me!"

Once we returned to the squadron, I owed a round of coffee for the formation. I had "lost my nerve" and pulled up first to avoid crashing into the white cliffs.

This was the challenge of the maneuver: Who would lose their nerve first and pull up over the cliffs?

Hypoxia

It Was Pouring Rain. The tower cleared me for takeoff as I taxied to Runway 21.

"Mission 4018 is cleared to Gütersloh via Oldenburg as requested, climb and maintain FL310."

I jotted down the clearance in my shorthand style, a method of symbols and essential numbers akin to how rally drivers note their route descriptions. To confirm my understanding, I repeated the clearance verbatim back to the tower. In case of radio failure during the flight, air traffic control would rely on my adherence to the confirmed instructions.

Visibility was poor; no contours were visible ahead. I could only orient myself to the sides, as though driving slowly through heavy rain without turning on the wipers. The preflight inspection, strapping in, and engine start in the rain were not only unpleasant - no one enjoys sitting in a wet seat - but turning on the cockpit heating system caused the canopy to fog up from the inside.

My wingman, Major Mathias Wilke, an experienced G.91 pilot, followed me along the taxiway.

"Two is up", Wilke confirmed on the new frequency - a check to ensure we were both tuned in.

We taxied onto the runway.

"Mission 4018 ready for takeoff," I radioed the tower.

"Two" had rolled up beside me on my left side.

"Mission 4018 is cleared for takeoff, contact departure."

"Roger, Mission 4018, channel 8, go."

"Two," responded Major Wilke.

I signaled to spool up the engines and pushed my throttle fully forward. The Orpheus engine slowly spooled up from 35% idle to 90%, then quickly surged to maximum power between 100% and 102%. I reduced the throttle to 95%, giving my wingman room to adjust between 95% and maximum power.

After another instrument check, engine parameters normal, radio compass aligned with runway heading, warning lights off, and oxygen system indicating proper flow, I glanced at my wingman. He nodded, confirming all his checks were complete.

I leaned my head back against the ejection seat, took a two-second pause, and nodded sharply to release the brakes. My wingman followed suit, adjusting his engine power to maintain position.

The cockpit blower cleared the moisture from the windshield as the slipstream pushed the rain away from the canopy. I pulled the stick back to achieve a 5° climb on the artificial horizon and held it steady. Both aircraft lifted off simultaneously.

I signaled the gear retraction with a circling hand motion. A confirming nod from Wilke, and I moved the gear lever up. "Thud-thud," the landing gear was up. Another nod, and we retracted the flaps together.

"Husum departure, Mission 4018 flight, good morning, airborne," I reported.

"Mission 4018 flight, continue as cleared," came the response from Departure Radar.

We entered the clouds, thick and black, as we pilots like to say: "Dark as a bear's ass."

The air became turbulent. My focus was on the instruments, with occasional glances in my rearview mirror, which I had angled to keep my wingman in sight without turning my head. A quick eye movement was enough.

The turbulence rattled us, but Wilke held a steady position just three feet off my wing. The clouds were so dense at times that I briefly lost sight of him, but I trusted he was there.

At 10,000 feet, I checked my oxygen gauge: "Full." The "blinker," a white indicator that moved with each breath, was functioning correctly.

"Mission 4018, cleared to level 310 direct to Oldenburg."

"Roger, direct Oldenburg, Mission 4018," I confirmed.

We climbed smoothly above the clouds, leaving the turbulent layer behind. My wingman now flew in loose formation, 50 meters away.

A Sudden Crisis

"Mission 4018 is level 310," I reported reaching the assigned cruising altitude.

"Mission 4018, maintain," came the confirmation.

Above the clouds, the changing patterns of light and shadow were mesmerizing. I let my gaze linger on the elegant silhouette of my wingman's aircraft. This was more than flying; it was an unspoken, perfect communication between two pilots who trusted each other with their lives, a symbiosis of man and machine.

Then, something changed. The clouds ahead brightened, and the sun's glare became almost overwhelming. I felt warm, too warm. My perception shifted dramatically. The light intensified, and even the cockpit instruments seemed to glow unnaturally bright.

I realized something was wrong. I fumbled for the microphone switch on the throttle.

G.91 R3 – Single Seater.

"Mission 4018 - 2, something's wrong. I think I have hypoxia."

I tried to switch my oxygen regulator to 100%, but my hand kept missing the knob. Finally, I managed to turn it.

"Mission 4018 Lead, I take the lead, stay loose," Wilke responded.

My wingman overtook me on the left and assumed formation lead. Through the haze of my disoriented mind, I vaguely heard his mayday call:

"Lippe Radar, Mission 4018, Mayday, Mayday, Mayday."

Following his commands, I continued to fly in formation, albeit on autopilot in my mind.

Awareness returned when I saw a runway ahead. Wilke signaled me to land and broke off to avoid obstructing the emergency response on the ground.

I landed safely at Oldenburg Air Base, where the fire brigade and flight surgeon were waiting. Following protocol, I shut down the engine and kept the canopy closed until the doctor gave the all-clear from a ladder.

Oxygen samples were taken immediately, followed by a blood test to rule out contamination or poisoning in the oxygen supply.

Wilke landed after a circuit and joined me on the ground.

The Cause

A tiny 2.5mm screw had worked loose from the oxygen mask mounted on my helmet, creating a small gap between the mask and my nose. This allowed cabin air, with insufficient oxygen for 20,000-foot pressure altitude, to mix with the oxygen supply. The resulting hypoxia worsened rapidly until we descended to denser air, which stabilized my blood oxygen levels.

The screw was replaced by R&S specialists at Oldenburg, and we returned back to our home base Husum.

This incident underscored the importance of hypoxia training in the altitude chamber. The experience reinforced why constant vigilance and preparation are critical for any pilot.

G.91 R3 of FBW 41 at Husum.

Fiat G-91R/3 of WaSlw 50 (Weaponschool 50) as it appeared during NATO exercise "Black-sky" in 1970.

Night flight

Night formation flights were a regular part of the training program, typically conducted toward the end of the conversion course. These flights were influenced by factors such as weather, night flying restrictions, training prerequisites, and various other considerations.

On this particular evening, thunderstorms were forecast over southern Germany. However, the storms were expected to be scattered enough to allow us to circumnavigate around them. Since the G.91 was not equipped with a weather radar, we had to rely on visual detection or radar support to avoid thunderstorm clouds.

Interestingly, the atmosphere in the squadron during night flights was always more subdued than during the day. Briefings were more detailed, attention was sharper, and personal notes on the upcoming night flight were taken with greater care.

During the general briefing, we reviewed the weather, mission plan, departure and approach sequences, and the operational status of airfields in our flight area. Some airfields were open for night operations, while others were available only as alternates. Emergency procedures were emphasized, especially critical scenarios at night, such as radio failure or, worst-case, a complete electrical failure. In such a situation, instruments could only be read using the flashlight carried for emergencies, and the landing gear could only be manually extended, while flaps and air brakes would not function.

The operations officer scheduled the flights well in time, so that there was always enough time to enjoy a leisurely cup of coffee before we left the squadron building. For some, it became a ritual, a quick game, playing cards of "Skat" or "Bavarian Schafkopf", while others lounged in chairs, quietly dozing.

Our group of four, two instructors and two trainees, gathered near the flight equipment room. We received our helmets, survival vests with emergency radios, leg restraints and flashlights. Grabbing our "goody packs" (inflight documents bag), we headed out loaded like packed mules to the aircraft.

After a thorough preflight inspection, I took my seat onto the front ejection seat, with my trainee, a WSO (Weapons Systems Officer) candidate, in the rear seat. We meticulously worked through the checklist, perhaps a paying a little more attention than during the day. I then signaled the ground crew with a circling motion of my finger to start the engine. Everything proceeded according to plan.

For the first half of the flight, we were "Fortuna lead", with the plan to switch formation lead to "Fortuna 2" for the return leg.

We taxied into position, and the tower cleared us for takeoff under Munich Radar control:

"Fortuna flight cleared takeoff runway 27. Have a nice trip."

I advanced the throttle to 100% and then eased it back to 95%, allowing "Fortuna 2" to match power. I waited for a clear nod from "Fortuna 2" to confirm readiness. If visibility made the nod difficult to discern, he would instead confirm readiness via radio: "Fortuna 2 ready."

Finally, after what felt like an eternity:

"Two ready."

"Fortuna flight standby brakes, brakes now."

At "now," we both released the brakes, and our aircraft accelerated. Reaching 120 knots, I gently pulled back on the stick, raising the nose to 5° above the horizon, and held that position. Out of the corner of my eye, I saw "Fortuna 2" maintaining position on my right side. At 150 knots, then 155 knots, we lifted off.

At night, we allowed slightly more time for stabilization before raising the gear, giving the wingman a couple of extra seconds to align in formation.

"Fortuna flight standby gear, gear now."

We raised the landing gear.

"Fortuna flight standby flaps, flaps now."

We retracted the flaps from their 70% takeoff position and flew into the cool darkness of the night.

Within minutes, we encountered thin wisps of cloud, which soon thickened, and we were enveloped in the cloud layer. The aircraft lights reflected in the clouds, creating an eerie glow that made the planes more visible. "Fortuna 2" turned off his red anti-collision beacon to minimize distraction.

At 18,000 feet, we were above the clouds. The sky was clear, with the horizon glowing in the fading hues of a sunset, dark reds fading into deep violet before disappearing into the blackness of the night.

As we flew between the town of Dinkelsbühl (TACAN CH125) and Frankfurt (TACAN CH58), we passed over a thunderstorm.

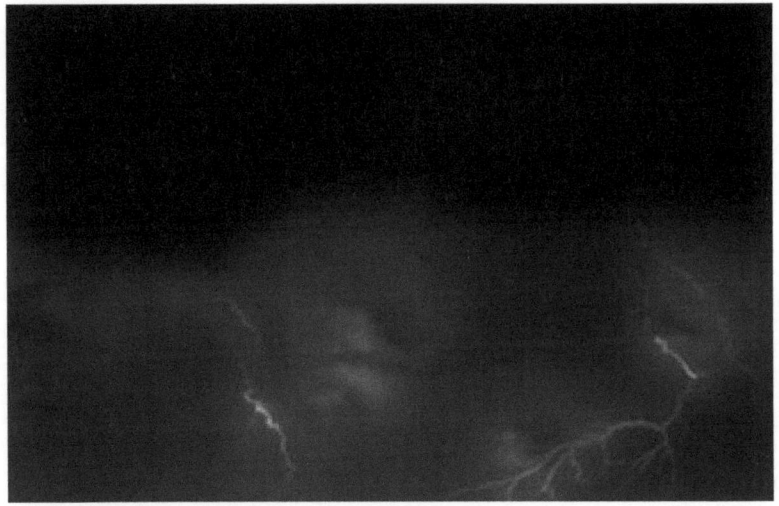

The sight was breathtaking, a memory that remains vivid to this day. At 31,000 feet, we were well above the storm, with the cloud tops at roughly 27,000 feet.

Lightning illuminated the clouds below us in a spectacular display of nature's power. Without the accompanying thunder, the storm lost its sense of menace and instead became a mesmerizing light show.

Lead Change

After halfway of our route, we executed a lead change. This maneuver was done via radio instructions:

"Fortuna flight, standby lead change."

As "Two," the wingman would drift about 30 feet outward to maintain visibility of the lead aircraft's outline and position lights. A slight power increase of 1-2% allowed a gradual move forward to align with the lead aircraft.

The flight leader would acknowledge:

"Fortuna 2, take lead."

"Fortuna 2" passed the lead aircraft, shifting focus from the leader's position to his own instruments. Meanwhile, the previous leader adjusted position to follow "Fortuna 2" in formation. "Fortuna 2 is leading."

The lead change was complete, and "Fortuna 2" guided the formation back to Fürstenfeldbruck.

After about an hour, we entered Fürstenfeldbruck's approach area, guided by Munich Radar into a descent. Switching to the airfield's Ground-Controlled Approach (GCA), we conducted a radar-assisted approach in formation.

At 200 feet above ground, where a visual transition would normally occur, we executed a formation go-around. Accelerating to 300 knots, and pulled up into the visual traffic pattern one by one to practice multiple night landings. This standard procedure allowed both the front-seat pilot and sometimes an Instructor Pilot in the rear cockpit to gain valuable practice.

After the final landing, we taxied to the parking area or into a shelter. The customary farewell to the tower followed:

"Fürsty tower, Fortuna, good night."

Interestingly, this "good night" was a tradition unique to night operations. A daytime flight rarely ended with a "good day."

The evening concluded with the ritual "Night Flight Beer" in the squadron lounge or Officers' Mess, a chance to relax, chat with air traffic controllers, and resolve any misunderstandings or tensions from the day's operations.

Backseat ride with the "Spillone"[11]

Comrades, this isn't Rainer's first flight in an "F-104G", but I'll still go over our planned flight in more details, said Stefano, my Italian Air Force pilot, as he began the briefing for our mission.

The four of us sat at the table - Stefano and I scheduled in the lead aircraft, and Mario and Filippo as "Two," our wingman. We had planned a low-level mission departing from my home airbase, Fürstenfeldbruck (EDSF), flying over the Nördlinger Ries to the Black Forest, and back to land in "Fürsty."

The 4° Stormo of the Italian Air Force was visiting our Fighter Bomber Wing (Jagdbombergeschwader) 49 for a squadron exchange. Alongside learning about each other's operational practices, we conducted joint training flights and had the opportunity to fly in each other's aircraft. The Italian pilots flew with us in the Alpha Jet and G.91 T3, as both aircraft were in service with us at the time. We, in turn, got to experience the Italian TF-104G "Starfighter".

"Our call sign is 'Leo 33.' I'm the flight lead, Rainer is flying with me in the backseat, and Mario and Filippo are "No. 2.".

Stefano then detailed the entire flight plan. We synchronized our watches, noted the aircraft tail numbers, ours was 4-33, and Mario and Filippo's was 4-31, and concluded the briefing with a discussion of potential emergencies. We reviewed contingency actions, nearby airfields along the route, their capabilities (radar approaches, arresting systems for hydraulic failures, etc.), and

---

[11]   The F-104G/S „Starfighter" was affectionately called „Spillone" (Pin) in Italy.

considered the possibility of worsening weather conditions over the Black Forest.

Twenty minutes later, the briefing was complete. We had time for a quick coffee before leaving the squadron building, laden with maps, flight logs, survival vests, G-suits, and helmets.

Stefano gave me a final orientation to the rear cockpit of the TF-104G, explaining which pins to pull to arm the ejection seat, the oxygen system, and how to lock the canopy. Stefano then completed the preflight check, settled into the cockpit, and a few minutes later, the startup unit roared to life, igniting the J-79 engine.

The standard takeoff weight of the TF-104G without weapons was approximately 10,000 kg, including 3,000 kg of JP-4 fuel. The J-79 engine, with nearly 23,000 horsepower in full afterburner, accelerated the aircraft to a liftoff speed of 190 knots - roughly 350 km/h. These values were approximate, as factors like air pressure, altitude, and temperature had to be accounted for.

At 190 knots, we lifted off.

We exited the control zone and tower frequency, heading east. "Leo 33 2" maintained a tactical formation, one-mile line abreast. At an altitude of 500 feet AGL and a cruising speed of 450 knots (833 km/h), we enjoyed perfect weather for the first half of the route, with a classical Bavarian sky, "white and blue" as described in the Bavarian anthem.

I didn't have to worry about flying or navigation. My Italian pilot allowed me to simply enjoy the 55-minute ride in the TF-104G, soaking in the stunning landscapes, the early morning ambiance, and the pure thrill of flying. As always, I had my camera with me.

I asked Mario, the pilot of our "No 2", to close the distance for some photos of the "Spillone" in flight, a nickname for the Italian TF-104G. After 30 minutes, the visibility at low altitude began to deteriorate as we approached a weather front moving in from the west over the Black Forest. The worsening conditions made our approach to the planned target, the "Kleine Kinzig Reservoir" at the eastern edge of the Black Forest, increasingly challenging.

We pulled up from low-level flight, navigating through gaps in the clouds. Sometimes we had brief ground visibility, but it would

TF-104G of the Italian Air Force.

quickly disappear again. "Leo 33 2" tightened formation to avoid losing sight of us. The flight was determined to strike the target, aiming for a successful training mission.

We repeatedly adjusted our altitude, threading through the clouds to maintain ground visibility for the last few minutes before the simulated attack on the reservoir. I watched "Leo 33 2" frequently correct its position to stay aligned with us.

"Leo 33 flight, weapons check" Stefano instructed. In our case, this meant simulating weapon activation.

The clouds pressed us lower, forcing us below 500 feet at 450 knots over the dense Black Forest. Stefano spotted a break in the

137

clouds, a valley opening up like a giant tube, with the reservoir dam visible at the far end. The cloud base prevented a glide bomb run; instead, we crossed the target and began our westbound return.

"Leo 33 2 is Bingo," came the call from our wingman. Mario had reached the minimum fuel reserve required to return to Fürsty, with enough fuel for a diversion to Lechfeld (EDSL) if necessary.

On the return leg, the weather improved as we approached eastern Bavaria. Twenty minutes later, we reached the "Ammersee", its northern tip serving as the designated entry point for the landing pattern.

After nearly 55 minutes, Stefano extended the landing gear at 260 knots. "Leo 33 2" followed at a safe distance, so we conducted individual landings instead of a formation landing. Stefano touched down on runway 09 at 160 knots, and Mario followed shortly after.

"Grazie, Stefano. Grazie, Mario and Filippo."

This flight remains a lasting memory, a flight shared with new friends from the 4º Stormo of the Aeronautica Militare.

Farewell

Our farewell flight in a G.91 was conducted in a trainer variant, the G.91 T3. All the single-seaters had already been decommissioned for scrapping, leaving only the 491st Squadron in "Fürsty" to train the last Weapons System Operators (WSOs) flying the remaining twin-seaters. Back then, WSOs were still called "Kampfbeobachter".

Fiat G.91 T3

In the Luftwaffe, there was a healthy rivalry, which included WSOs with the introduction of two-seater combat aircraft. In the Royal Air Force, they were known as "navigators," reflecting one of their primary roles: to assist and alleviate the workload of the pilot.

In the small book "London Flights 1917", Lieutenant Walter Aschoff described his journey to becoming an "observer" in military aviation.

As an infantryman and army officer deployed to the frontline during World War I, he wrote after just four weeks:

"I increasingly grow into a flier, adopting the expressions, manners, and traditions of this 'class', sharing with many young officers the sole desire to be promptly assigned to a unit for frontline duty."[12]

Later, after Lieutenant Aschoff and his pilot, Lieutenant Böckelwang, made a forced landing in fields and meadows about 30 kilometers northeast of Brussels, he noted in his diary:

"The phrases that followed from my pilot, I wish to omit here - both for the honor of the observer corps and my own sake. The 'marriage' that had been solemnly entered into with such great expectations the day before, had already suffered a crack."[13]

It seems, not much has changed since 1917. Over time, the role of the "observer" has once again become "obsolete." Fourth- and fifth-generation aircraft like the F-16, Eurofighter, Rafale, F-22, and F-35 are all single-seaters.

A Farewell in Two Ways

This flight was a double farewell. It marked our final flight in a Fiat G.91 and the end of the Luftwaffe's WSO training program. In the future the WSO training would take place in the U.S. Air Force.

On January 4, 1982, under a sunny winter sky, we walked across the flight line in Fürsty to our assigned aircraft, tail number 34+18. This was our last flight in a G.91 T3. On the same day, the squadron conducted its final training flight with the G.91.

A Sentimental Goodbye

I felt a twinge of sadness. The G.91 had been a familiar companion, and I loved flying it, even as a flight instructor. Of course, it was no longer "state of the art", its technology, performance, and avionics belonged to the second generation of fighter aircraft. Remarkably, only 14 years separated the maiden flight of the Me 262 in July 1942 and the Fiat G.91 in August 1956.

---

12   Walter Aschoff: "Londonflüge 1917", p. 10.

13   Ibid, p. 12.

I prepared a flight plan for our last flight with care and approached it with a sense of nostalgia. In the rear cockpit sat "Hans," a fellow instructor pilot in Fürsty. At 1:30 p.m., I released the brakes.

Our planned low-level flight took us westward, cruising at 500 feet AGL and a standard speed of 360 knots. Just before passing "Augsburg", I climbed to 1,500 feet to reduce noise over the southern parts of the city. On the western outskirts, I descended again to 500 feet, maintaining this altitude "more or less precisely" for the remainder of the low-level route.

Occasionally, I banked into a turn, pushing the throttle to 95% to maintain speed through 4-5g maneuvers. It was pure exhilaration to roll the aircraft nearly inverted, the canopy skimming hillsides and trees, diving into the next valley.

The winter landscape beneath me was breathtaking, viewed from the inverted perspective of a cockpit, a final love letter to my years in the G.91.

High-Altitude play

The second half of the flight brought us into TRA-207, an airspace reserved for military aircraft at altitudes between 10,000 and 25,000 feet. Within the airspace, pilots were responsible for avoiding midair collisions. Munich Radar provided only advisory warnings for aircraft not part of the same formation.

I initiated a gentle descent, pushed the throttle to 95%, and at 480 knots, pulled back on the stick for a looping maneuver. Inverted at 16,000 feet, I saw the wings cutting across the horizon, a fleeting, awe-inspiring moment. I checked my airspeed - 190 knots - and let the nose fall.

I followed with a barrel roll, then a few quick rolls, before pulling into an Immelmann turn. On my back at 200 knots, I leveled briefly before executing a Split-S. The vibrations in the control stick, the wing shudders at high g-forces, and the distinct smell of the aircraft, a blend of hot hydraulic oil, JP-4 fuel, and cabin air, created an intimate connection with the G.91.

As I left the reserved airspace and set course for the "Ammersee", the engine still running at 95%, I reached 520 knots. Flying along the lake's western edge, the white radomes and parabolic antennas of Raisting came into view.

Banking left, I steered toward the middle of the lake, briefly inverted one last time, and reduced throttle to 83%, slowing to 300 knots for the approach to "Point A." Passing Stegen on my right, I entered the traffic pattern.

A Final Landing

At the imagined touchdown point above the runway, I banked 60° left into the downwind leg. Landing gear down, flaps set, landing lights on. At 155–160 knots, I descended for the final approach to runway 27.

Last 4-ship formation with the "Old Lady".

For a few extra minutes in the air, I requested a touch-and-go maneuver. After a steep climb and tight turn, I repeated the landing sequence.

Finally, at 135 knots, the tires kissed the tarmac. I deployed the drag chute, slowing the aircraft. Turning onto the taxiway, I jettisoned the chute and taxied to the parking area.

The crew chief waited with the ladder in hand.

For the last time, I shut down the Orpheus engine, it had never let me down. Before returning to the squadron, I ran my hand along the fuselage, tracing the intake.

It was January 4, 1982, at 2:20 p.m. Fifty minutes after takeoff, I knew I'd never fly her again.

Alpha Jet

In 1966, the German Ministry of Defense tasked the domestic aerospace industry with designing a trainer aircraft to replace the aging T-33 and Fouga Magister. The need for such a trainer was projected for the mid-1970s.

Around the same time, the French Air Force ("Armée de l'Air") issued a similar call for the development of a training aircraft.

Following the Luftwaffe's decision to conduct all jet pilot training in the United States using T-37 "Tweet" and T-38 "Talon" aircraft, there remained an urgent requirement for a replacement for the aging Fiat G.91. In 1969, France and Germany agreed to jointly develop an aircraft for training and close air support. The Luftwaffe planned to adopt this aircraft as the successor to the G.91.

Initially, a production run of 200 aircraft was envisioned for each nation.

The joint project narrowed the competition to two promising designs: Dassault-Bréguet's Br-126 concept from France and Dornier's P-375 proposal

Le "Larzac" et une de ses nombreuses applications...

Bréguet Br.126 Alpha Jet mock-up - "Aviation Magazine International" - No. 516 - June 15, 1969

from Germany. These two projects were merged to create the TA-501 designation (375 + 126).

Thus, the TA-501 "Alpha Jet" project was born.

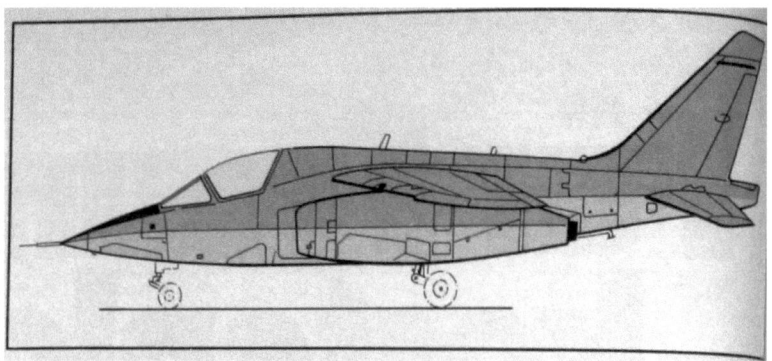

Unofficial artist rendering of a single-seat Alpha Jet, from "Flug-Revue" 01/1976

The Luftwaffe eventually procured a total of 175 Alpha Jets[14] for its three fighter-bomber wings (Jagdbombergeschwader) 41, 43, and 49, as well as the Luftwaffe Training Range Command in Beja, Portugal.

Upon re-equipping, these units retained their original roles from the G.91 era: close air support, battlefield interdiction, and the engagement of enemy ground forces. Additionally, the JaboG 41 was tasked with combating enemy naval forces in coastal regions.

A new mission was also outlined: counter-helicopter operations. However, this role never advanced beyond the testing phase and a specialized component of the weapons instructor training.

On January 8, 1980, JaboG 49 received its first Alpha Jets. By the end of May 1980, the Luftwaffe Training Range Command in Beja,

---

14   Nicknames for the Alpha Jet included "Alfi," "NATO Moped," "Laughing Dove," "Air Moped," "Alphons," and " Combat Vacuum Cleaner." These names, however, were coined not by pilots but by "non-pilots" on the ground!

Portugal, had received its Alpha Jets to commence training and conversion flights.

Alpha Jet formation returning from "Coca Range" near Lisbon.

For a comprehensive overview of the Alpha Jet weapons system, refer to the book "Alpha Jet" by Bernd Vetter and Frank Vetter.

Low level flying.

Tamila

Lisboa, the city of Saudade, Fadistas, Ginjas, Bagaços, Gambas, Meninas, Mulheres, the Beixa, and, alongside all that, the "Tamila." One of our Lieutenants, an "insider" at the Tamila, suggested a spontaneous weekend flight to Lisbon. We weren't allowed to land at "Lisbon International Airport," but there was a military airfield nearby: Montijo. It was located on the other side of the Tagus River and easily accessible by ferry.

Our flight took us directly from Fürstenfeldbruck to Montijo. My fellow pilot knew Montijo airfield as well as he knew the Tamila. A confirmed bachelor, he had a particular appreciation for Lisbon's nightlife.

The forecasted weather for landing in Montijo was "Blue+," meaning a visibility of more than 8 km and less than 3/8 cloud cover below 2,500 feet. South of the Pyrenees, the sky was entirely cloudless.

We descended from our cruising altitude of 35,000 feet, spotting Portugal's coastline and shortly after, Lisbon and the military airfield east of the city.

T3 of the "Esqadra 301 Jaguares"

"Lisboa Radar, GAF 4277 cancel IFR, going Montijo Tower for visual approach."

I informed Lisbon Radar as we descended below 10,000 feet. "GAF 4277, cleared to leave for Montijo Tower 267.9", came the reply from Lisbon Radar.

South of Lisbon lies the district of Almada, connected to the city by the "25 de Abril Bridge," named after the "Carnation Revolution" on April 25, 1974. Overlooking Lisbon is "Cristo Rei",

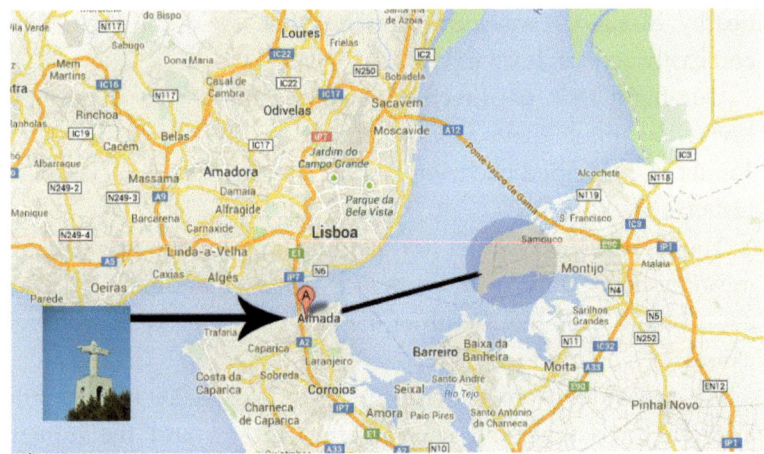

Map excerpt from Google Maps.

the statue of Christ that watches over the Portuguese capital. Some playful voices said "Cristo Rei" pointed the way to Montijo with his outstretched arms, while more irreverent ones claimed, "He's showing us the way to the Tamila."

Montijo was the home to the "Jaguares Squadron", Esqadra 301, which was still flying the Fiat G.91 at the time. Ground support was fully provided by their technicians, who took over our aircraft upon arrival. After a warm welcome at the Jaguares Squadron, we caught up with familiar faces we would meet again over the years at legendary pilot parties in Beja or Monte Real.

After the obligatory cup of coffee, we slung our bags over our shoulders and set off for Lisbon. A short ferry ride across the Tagus brought us to the city, where we checked into our hotel, showered, sprayed on a few spritzes of Eau de Cologne, and donned casual attire. Then it was off to the "feeding alley," Lisbon's famed street for its original and excellent restaurants.

Around 10:00 p.m., we stepped into the Tamila, and who did we meet at the bar even before ordering our first "Cerveja"? Two Portuguese G.91 pilots!

My colleague later told me that the Tamila[15] had practically served as a "Second O-Club" for some Portuguese Air Force officers at the time. Apparently, it wasn't much different in 1917.[16]

"Rita" and "Marisa" introduced themselves as the pilots' girlfriends. Before we knew it, the two charming daughters of Guinea-Bissau were sitting with us, sipping Superbock, and teaching us some fun Portuguese phrases.

Obrigado por uma grande noite.

On Monday morning at 9:30 a.m., we pushed the throttles to 100% and took off toward Bordeaux, a frequently used refueling stop on flights from Portugal or Spain back to Germany.

The rest of the flight was routine.

---

[15]   Nightclub Tamila, Lisboa, Av. Duque de Loulé 69. As of 2020, the club can still be found on Facebook under "Tamila Club for Adult Entertainment.

[16]   Ricco Pizzini, "Through!", 1917, p. 29.

Torremolinos Again

Among the Spanish military airfields like Getafe, Valencia, and Madrid-Torrejón, Málaga was one of our preferred landing spots. Málaga Airport was located close to Torremolinos, one of Spain's largest tourist hubs. Over time, Torremolinos has become, in my view, one of Europe's less inviting hotel zones.

The airport was a civilian facility with a small "corner" at the western end of the runway designated as a "military section." This area included a refueling truck, a flight operations office, a weather advisor, and a phone, nothing more, but nothing more was needed. On a Friday, we would secure our aircraft ourselves, and by Monday morning, we would ready them for takeoff again. The only requirement was a Spanish ground crew member standing by with a fire extinguisher during engine startup.

In the early 1980s, on a Monday morning as we prepared our planes for the return flight to our home base, I noticed an "Ilyushin Il-62" from East Germany's "Interflug" fleet not far away.

"I'm going to say hello," I called out to my fellow pilots and marched directly toward the Il-62. Why it was parked in Málaga, I couldn't explain then or now, as East German citizens were effectively "locked in" at that time, and a vacation in Málaga was virtually unthinkable.

Confidently, I strode across the large tarmac toward the East German aircraft, noting crew members nearby. But as soon as I set my foot on the first step of the gangway, I was sharply yelled at. Neither my greeting nor my pleasantries were acknowledged. To them, I was the "class enemy," and approaching the plane was strictly off-limits.

Unfortunately, I didn't take a photo of the Il-62 at the time. Had I included the crew in a photograph, I'd likely have been internationally pursued by the STASI as a "spy."

I slowly walked back across the scorching tarmac, shimmering with heat, toward our Alpha Jets. My fellow pilots laughed at my friendly approach and bluntly remarked that they hadn't expected any different behavior from the East German pilots.

A few years later, former NVA (National People's Army) pilots were flying combat and transport aircraft for the Luftwaffe and were welcomed as comrades into our ranks. Of course, those who flew to Spain in the 1980s were likely not among the most ideologically loyal party pilots.

We taxied both aircraft onto runway 13, requesting clearance for takeoff and a right turn to fly low-level to Valencia, crossing the Sierra Nevada mountains.

"Málaga tower, GAF 4149 requests taxi."

"GAF 4149, cleared to taxi runway 31," the tower replied.

"Málaga tower, GAF 4149 requests a right turn after takeoff and low-level departure direct to Valencia."

"Negative, you are cleared for a left turn after takeoff, enroute to Valencia."

This was not what our flight leader had in mind, he had promised the "girls from the weekend" they'd see our jets flying over the beach one last time. A "very relaxed" right turn would have taken us over the beachfront in front of the hotel. Instead, we were forced into a left turn toward the mountains.

Promises, however, are promises.

"Málaga tower, GAF 4149 ready for takeoff."

"GAF 4149, cleared for takeoff runway 13, adios."

"GAF 4149 flight channel 12 go",

"Two".

On Channel 12, we were able to communicate between the two

Low, low, low to Torremolinos.

aircraft. Our "relaxed left turn" did, after all, take us over the beach at Torremolinos, where our German weekend acquaintances enthusiastically waved their beach towels.

However, we kept it to a single flyby over the beach at "Torre" and then disappeared into the valleys of the Sierra Nevada.

Diving into a valley of the Sierra Nevada in Spain.

Striptease in the Squadron Command Post

Carnival was, after all, Carnival, even if it was called "Fasching" in Bavaria, whether celebrated in a pub or in the squadron command post known as the "Bw50."

In the 1980s, we celebrated enthusiastically, often together with our wives, fiancées, and girlfriends. The squadron command post provided a perfect venue for a Carnival party: first, it was a "restricted area within a restricted area"; second, it was windowless; and third, it was soundproof. The duty officer was tasked with hiring a proper stripper for the occasion, and he was "personally" responsible, to take care of her. I recall him personally escorting the "dancer" to the command post and ensuring that "Josephine" was safely delivered back to her home early the next morning.

Carnival in our Command Post.

Josephine.

As with most tasks and orders in the military - if not all - our Lieutenant had this "artist" formally contracted well in advance. Her "Manager," the man without his permission she certainly would not have performed, signed on her behalf. The operations officer's control cell was transformed into a dressing room, while the briefing room doubled as a dance floor and stage.

At the time, 38 years ago, a Lieutenant didn't lose much sleep over moral consequences. Nearly 40 years later, a duty officer would likely face significant consequences for organizing such an event.

Interestingly, even the women attending had no objections back then. On the contrary, they spoke for some time afterward about what a great Carnival-Party it had been.

Carnival was, after all, Carnival - and in the 1980s, it was allowed to be a little risqué.

Traditions

For me, flying fighters isn't just a career,
it's a way of life.
Any of my cohorts will tell you that.
Being a part of this exclusive
fraternity changes your outlook on
life and leaves a deep mark upon
your soul.
The Fighter Pilot's Lifestyle is one steeped in
Tradition. New members of this
unique circle must learn its history
and carry on its traditions, for they
will be the ones to instill pride in the
future generations of pilots that follow them.
                    Robert Aschenbrener, Capt. USAF[17]

The established traditions of fighter pilots have come under scrutiny in recent years. The fighter pilots of the Korean War, the Vietnam War, or the Cold War were rarely guided by "political correctness." However, the "military leadership" of all Air Forces consistently upheld more refined views, demonstrating behavior and morals that were mature and, indeed, exemplary.

Young fighter pilots carried on the traditions of older pilots with passion. Many of these traditions trace their roots back to the early days of military aviation, particularly within the "Royal Flying Corps".

The traditions of German pilots from 1910 to 1918 primarily revolved around the decoration of their own aircraft. In the early years, the emerging Air Forces afforded pilots some creative freedom. The quintessential "British aviation traditions" were later

---

[17]   „Asch" Aschenbrener was Squadron Commander of the 7th
         Fighter Squadron. He flew 345 combat missions. The USAF 7th
         Fighter Squadron was 2014 deactivated.

adopted by American aviators and subsequently passed on to NATO Air Forces. For example, songs, games, and quirks originally British migrated to the Americans and then back to Europe and the Luftwaffe. This was undoubtedly aided by the shared aviation language of English and the social evenings at the bars of officers clubs across NATO Air Forces.

Many traditions evolved over time, while others were consciously altered. Some rituals and customs were explicitly banned, either by their own military leadership or even by the "political class."

Notable examples include the "Tailhook Scandal" of the U.S. Navy[18] or the "purge" of the U.S. Air Force in 2012, during which all offices, computers,

Song book of the 77th Fighter Squadron.

and hard drives were searched for politically incorrect content. As is often the case with similar actions, some "babies were thrown out with the bathwater."

This purge was prompted by the complaint of a former female Sergeant regarding the content of an "Unofficial Songbook" from the U.S. Air Force's "77th Fighter Squadron". It is undisputed that some lyrics in this "Combat Songbook", as in many other "Fighter

---

18   William H. McMichael – "The Mother Of All Hooks: The Story of the U.S. Navy's Tailhook Scandal

Pilot Songbooks,"[19] were provocative, borderline, or even outright distasteful.

However, if we evaluate these lyrics retrospectively, we might consider them **in the context of their time**. Many of the song lyrics originated during the Vietnam War. For example, here's a text from the "USAF F-105" pilots during that era:

From hooch in Southeast Asia,
To the place aces dwell,
To the Strip Club down in Zuke,
We know so well.

Sing the fighter jocks assembled,
With their glasses raised on high,
Sing they poorly, not to clearly,
Loud as well.

We will throw our glasses wildly,
And throw our bombs as well,
And the finks in Two A.D.[20]
Can go to hell.

What has never changed - and hopefully never will - is the mindset of the fighter pilots. The men and women who sit in the cockpits today remain performance-driven, characterized by a relentless pursuit of success. This mindset is aptly captured in the lyrics of a "Fighter Pilot Song" by Lt. Col. (Ret.) Dick Jonas of the U.S. Air Force:

---

[19]   Cold War Fighter Pilots Songbook

[20]   2nd Air Division.

The Last Fighter Pilot

Lyrics by Chip Dockery

He was born in the skies over France back in 1916,
a daring young man in a flimsy ole flying machine,
ed Rickenbacker, the Baron, Frank Luke, and the rest,
paving the high road for those who would follow the quest.

Chorus

In the '20s and '30s he stood against short-sighted men,
who clipped back his wings saying they'll never need him again.
Then he strapped on a spitfire and climbed through the bright
English blue,
to the cheers of the many who owed so much to the few,
from the white cliffs of Dover to islands of jungle and sand,
a whole world at war, but for him it was man against man.

Chorus

And when it was over, he stood against short-sighted men,
who clipped back his wings saying they'll never need him again.
Then he climbed in a Sabre and flew through the Korean sky,
up to Mig Alley with courage to fight and to die,
in Southeast Asia, he called down the thunder again,
but this one was different, they wouldn't allow him to win.

Chorus

And when it was over, he listened to short-sighted men,
who said it was his fault, and they'd never need him again,
The last Fighter Pilot is just like the first of his kind,
and when duty calls, he's the first to step over the line,
a child of the heavens, a grandson and son of the best,

still riding the high road and trying to follow the quest.

Chorus

In the twenty-first century, he stands against short-sighted men,
who'll clip back his wings when they think they don't need him.
Again,
for you self-serving bastards who kill with the stroke of a pen,
he stands at the ready, for the day that you need him again.

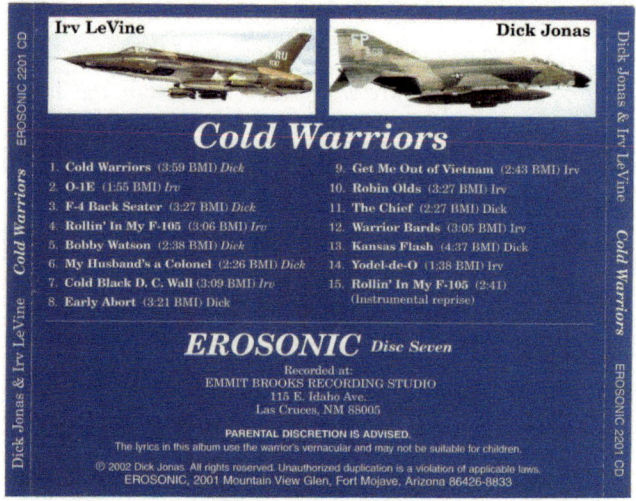

Dick Jonas, LtCol ret. USAF a great "Balladeer" for
"Fighter Pilot Songs".

Famous was the CD ....

" A Night at the Bar with the Boys"
.... a Fighter Pilot Songfest ....

It was recorded in "St. Thomas Church" in Scotland. Pilots from the
"509th Tactical Fighter Squadron" in Alconbury also happened to

160

be talented a cappella singers. The second song on the CD, "I Love My Wife", with lyrics far less romantic than the title suggests, was sung not only at the Alconbury bar. If you Google it, you can find the entire CD online. The CD, "The TLP Experience", was a continuation of this genre.

Songs that touched the Soul

A Military Service without songs has never existed. Aviators have always enjoyed singing, as evidenced by the numerous songbooks and preserved songs of fighter pilots. Unfortunately, the songs of soldiers from the years 1933 to 1945 were politically misused, and songs that once fostered camaraderie acquired a somber undertone - justifiably so.

With the integration of the German Air Force ("Luftwaffe") into NATO, the training of pilots and combat observers, later WSOs, in the USA, and the close bonds and friendships between NATO Air Force squadrons, English became the language of aviation. English-language aviator songs, predominantly from the UK and the USA, began to dominate the repertoire sung within aviation units. This shift was also likely influenced by the "Zeitgeist", as English-language songs were increasingly prevalent in everyday life.

Today, when "Old Aviators" gather to reminisce about their comrades, wild parties, NATO exercises, and the accompanying "Happy Hours," they often recall their "Fighter Pilot Songs", aviator songs that made their way into the German Air Force from the Royal Air Force (RAF) and the USAF.

The oldest known "Fighter Pilot Song" is believed to be "The Bold Aviator", which was popular among British aviators as early as 1912, when the British Flying Corps was first established. It was sung in every squadron and officers mess of the "Royal Flying Corps", the predecessor of the Royal Air Force, between 1914 and 1918. The melody of "The Tarpaulin Jacket" served as the basis for a parody, and the lyrics evolved over time, often adapted by pilots to reflect their mood or circumstances.

THE BOLD AVIATOR
or
THE DYING AIRMANN

Oh, the bold aviator was dying,
And as 'neath the wreckage he lay, he lay,
To the sobbing mechanics about him,
These last parting words he did say:

Chorus: Two valve springs you'll find in my stomach,
Three spark plugs are safe in my lung (my lung),
The prop is splinters inside me,
To fingers the joy-stick has clung.

Oh, had I the wings of a little dove,
Far away, far away would I fly,
Straight to the arms of my true love,
And there would I lay me and die.

Another version of the era:

A poor aviator lay dying,
At the end of a bright summer's day,
His comrades had gathered about him,
To carry his fragments away.

> **There are old Aviators,**
> **and bold Aviators,**
> **but no old and bold Aviators.**

The dawn of military aviation was an adventure for a unique reason, at the start, there were no binding regulations! This quickly changed as the aviation corps was soon forced into the constraints of service regulations, and pilots expressed their frustration in songs they sang over beers at the bar.

On June 20, 1941, the "US Army Air Corps" and the "GHQ Air Force" were officially transformed into the "United States Army Air Forces" through the implementation of "Army Regulation 95-5". General Henry Harley "Hap" Arnold was the commanding officer responsible for this transition.

In one of the popular "Fighter Pilot Songs", Arnold was humorously referenced in connection with the endless stream of new regulations. Pilots viewed these rules as restrictions on their freedom of flight, feeling they could no longer determine, or rather, "fly" at their limits on their own.

Glory Flying Regulations

Hap Arnold[21] built a fighting team that sang a fighting song,
about the Wild Blue Yonder & the days when men were strong,
but now we're regulated so we don't know right from wrong,
..... the force is shot to hell.

Chorus: Glory flying regulations,
have them read at all the stations.
Burn the ass of those that breaks them,
the force is shot to hell.

We flew B-26's through a hail of flak,
& bloody dying pilots gave their lives to bring 'em back,
now they're playing Ping-Pong in the operations shack,
the force is shot to hell.

I have seen them in their T-Bolts when their eyes were dancing flame,
I've seen their screaming power-dives that blasted Goering's name,

---

[21]   General Hap Arnold, founder of the USAF.

now they fly like sissies & they hang their heads in shame,
the force is shot to hell.

Now, one day I buzzed an airfield with another happy chap,
we flew a hot formation with my wingtip on his lap,
so they passed a new directive & we'll have no more of that,
the force is shot to hell.

So, now mine eyes are dim with tears for happy days of old,
we loved to take our chances for our hearts were young & bold,
from now on we have no choice but live to be quite old,
the force is shot to hell.

Pushing personal limits in flight, even at the risk of one's life, was a widely accepted reality. The prevailing "aviation spirit" was believed to be under threat.

In 1917, Lieutenant Walter Aschoff wrote in his memoirs "London Flights 1917", reflecting on the early years of military aviation:

"In our airmen's home, we maintained and nurtured strong camaraderie within the squadron and with neighboring units. In bad weather, cheerful banquets were held. A rough, but nonetheless heartfelt, wartime tone prevailed, and new arrivals quickly acclimated to it. Cheerful spirits, paired with a certain recklessness, were always at home with us aviators. No misfortune, no matter how tragic, could bring us down. When the order to take off came, whether by day or in the middle of the night, every man stepped up and did his duty."

By day, we flew together; by night, we drank and sang.
Jo Rammer, Starfighter Pilot[22]

---

[22]   Quoted from "Mach 2" by Rolf Stünkel, Page 91.

Since 1947, the USAF has even had its own anthem:

The Wild Blue Yonder

Off we go into the wild blue yonder,
Climbing high into the sun;
Here they come zooming to meet our thunder,
At 'em boys, Give 'er the gun! (Give 'er the gun now!)
Down we dive, spouting our flame from under,
Off with one heckuva roar!
We live in fame or go down in Flame.
Hey! Nothing'll stop the U.S. Air Force!

Minds of men fashioned a crate of thunder,
Sent it high into the blue,
Hands of men blasted the world asunder,
How they lived God only knew!
Souls of men dreaming of skies to conquer,
Gave us wings ever to soar,
With scouts before and bombers galore, Hey!
Nothing'll stop the US Air Force!

Here's a toast to the host of those,
Who love the vastness of the sky,
To a friend we send a message,
Of his brother men who fly.
We drink to those who gave their all of old,
Then down we roar,
to score the rainbow's pot of gold.
A toast to the host of men we boast, the US Air Force.
Off we go into the wild sky yonder,
Keep the wings level and true!
If you'd live to be a grey-haired wonder,
Keep your nose out of the blue! (Out of the blue, boy!)

Flying men guarding the nation's border,
We'll be there, followed by more,
In echelon we carry on! Hey!
Nothing'll stop the US Air Force!

"The Wild Blue Yonder" became synonymous with the place of longing for aviators - alongside the bar in the Officers' Club. "Yonder" implies farther than merely "up there," yet still within sight. The concept is metaphorical: "I know I am up there, and I will return."

Since the days of the Army Air Corps, "The Wild Blue Yonder" has been a steadfast term. It is also frequently found as a book title.

Tambourine of the Salvation Army.
Photo from the internet.

With the early success of the airplane as a reconnaissance tool and later as a military weapon system, an irresistible and romantic image of the aviator emerged, the conqueror of the third dimension, the warrior above the battlefield. To "fly" in that era meant to draw circles across the blue firmament, hide behind the clouds, and "come out of the sun."

During the Korean War, one particular aviator song gained immense popularity, tracing its origin to a Salvation Army hymn from 1915. In the early 20th century, when the Salvation Army in the USA sought donations on the streets and in front of

167

universities, they used an upturned tambourine to collect offerings from listeners, singing, "Throw a Nickel[23] on the drum, and you'll be saved."

In 1954, during his wartime deployment in Korea at Airbase K-14, F-86 pilot William Starr noted down the lyrics of frequently sung limericks in "The Fighter Pilot's Hymn Book". Starr later connected with "Military Folk Singer" Oscar Brand and shared the 238 song lyrics he had recorded in his notebook. In 1959, Oscar Brand selected a collection of these songs for a new album, with "Throw a Nickel on the Grass..." as the opening track. Oscar Brand made this song nearly immortal as an aviator anthem. It became one of the most beloved and frequently sung tunes at aviator bars:

Save A Fighter Pilot's Ass

Chorus:
Sing hallelujah, sing hallelujah,
Throw a Nickel on the Grass, save a fighter pilot's ass,
Sing hallelujah, sing hallelujah,
Throw a Nickel on the Grass, and you'll be saved.

I was cruising down the Yalu, doing 6 and 24,
when a call came from the Major, "Oh won't you save me, Sir.
Got three flak holes in my wingtips and my tanks ain't got no gas,
Mayday Mayday mayday, I got six MiGs on my ass."

Chorus:

---

[23] Throw a nickel..."references Greek mythology. Charon, the ferryman of the River Styx, transported the dead from the world of the living to the underworld. Payment in the form of a coin was required, placed under the tongue of the deceased. Souls without proper burial and the necessary fare were left stranded on the Styx's banks, doomed to a miserable existence. "Throw a nickel..."!

I shot my traffic pattern, and to me, it looked all right,
the air speed read 130, I really racked it tight,
then the airframe gave a shutter, the engine gave a wheeze,
Mayday Mayday Mayday, spin instructions please.

Chorus:

It was Split-S on my bomb run, and I got too goddamned low,
but I pressed that bloody button, and I let those babies go,
sucked the stick back fast as blazes, when I hit a high speed stall,
now, I won't see my mother, when the works all done next fall.

Chorus:

Then they sent me down to Pyongyang, the brief said, "no ack ack",
by the time that I arrived there, my wings was mostly flak,
then my engine coughed and sputtered, it was too cut up to Fly
Mayday Mayday Mayday, I'm too young to die.

Chorus:

I bailed out from the Sabre, and the landing came out fine,
with my E and E equipment, I made for our front line,
then I opened up my ration, to see what was in it,
the goddamned Quartermaster, why he filled the tin with grit.

The Vietnam War shaped an entire generation of U.S. Air Force pilots. The following song became a staple in the Officers' Clubs (O-Clubs) across Southeast Asia. Originally from the time of the British-Indian War, the lyrics were once again adapted to reflect the sentiments of the pilots during the Vietnam War:

Stand to Your glasses steady.[28]

Stand to your glasses steady,
this world is a world full of lies.
A toast to the dead already,
hurrah for the next man to die.

Chorus:
We are the boys who fly high in the sky,
bosom buddies while boozin' are we.
We are the boys that they send out to die,
bosom buddies while boozin' are we.
Up in headquarters they scream and the shout,
about lots of things they know nothing about.
But we are the boys they send out to die,
bosom buddies while boozin' are we.

"Pilots Are Victors" was the title of one of the aviation songs in the German language from the early days of military aviation.

Flieger sind Sieger.

Wir jagen durch die Lüfte,
wie Wotans wildes Heer.
Wir schaun die Wolkenklüfte,
und brausen übers Meer.

Wo tragen uns die Schwingen,
wohl über Berg und Tal.
Wenn die Propeller singen,
im ersten Morgenstrahl.

Flieger sind Sieger,
sind alle Zeit bereit.
Flieger sind Sieger.

In the skies, there were no trenches, no mud, no blood, no eyes of an opponent frozen in death. Those who died simply crashed. Others on the ground handled the aftermath. There were only successful pilots: "Richthofens," "Bishops," "Rickenbackers," and later "Gallands" and "Olds," and their impressive aircraft could be found in the "Wild Blue Yonder." They shot down planes in one-vs-one combat, dropped bombs on targets, flew back to the airfield, and were celebrated as "Flying Aces" with champagne and whiskey at the bar. The pilot was the "showpiece of the military," initially for the "Air Corps" and later for the Air Forces. They adorned their planes with personal symbols, painted them brightly, and sometimes decorated them with Pin-Up Girls.

For those who perceived the Air Force this way, a closer look was warranted.

In reality, these were dangerous missions, often fatal flights loaded with bombs and ammunition. On the ground, flak batteries waited; from the sun, the enemy pilot sought to shoot you down. The losses were exorbitantly high. A pilot began his career as a "golden boy" until he was shot down or crashed in bad weather. Many met their end during landings, or their engine failed mid-flight over a vast forest. And if the enemy pilot or flak didn't kill them, it was altitude sickness or frostbite. From this perspective, the conditions of war in the skies were just as miserable and wretched as those in the trenches on the ground.

Flying and Women

The officers' mess and the "girls at the bar" occasionally made all the difference.

**"An old pilot is one who can remember,
when flying was dangerous and sex was safe."**

Flying and eroticism have seemingly been intertwined since the first "leap into the air" - more than a century ago. Willy Hahn, one of the first German aviators, wrote about the everyday life of pilots in Berlin-Johannisthal in 1913/1914:

"We lived day to day, hand to mouth. Champagne binges and feasts, nights spent drinking, days spent sleeping. And if drinking were the only vice! The worst were the women. They were crazy about the pilots, flocking to the airfield, going from hand to hand. Yes, these women, they were the cause of so much misfortune. They were brought in from the Lindenkasino, the 'Palais de Danse', the old ballrooms. In the city, they demanded heavy sums, but out here, they gave everything for free, so enamored were they with their 'black devils'. But they drained the life from many a joyful young man, sapping the marrow from his bones and the sense from his brain. Sharp, steady eyes became dull, and when it came time to stand again outside in danger, to face the elements in battle, the nerves gave out. Many gave up this heavy, serious profession in time when they felt they could no longer do it. I have stood by many a coffin. When the catastrophic accident was discussed, I and others knew better. It was the women, the damned women."

And he continued:

"Not long ago, I had a long debate with an older naval officer. I spoke with him about the rapid aging of so many of our aviation officers and remarked how many were ruined prematurely. Surely flying had a devastating impact on the nervous system. He looked at me for a while and then said": *"You know, let's be honest. What ruins our young*

aviation officers the most is not the flying; it's the Johannisthal aviation lifestyle - it's the Johannisthal women."

"And in silence, I could not disagree with him. For many, many of my acquaintances, his words rang true. But it was peculiar, psychologically peculiar. Even more so in France than in Germany, I have observed this eerie connection between aviation and eroticism. It was as though the aviator had pledged his soul to the devil's woman, as though she determined the span of his life remaining."[24]

Loving couple above the clouds – Postcard from 1912

In 1944, the Luftwaffe issued a gunnery manual for aviators, signed by General of Fighter Pilots Adolf Galland[25] with the note on page 2: "Do not take this on combat missions".

---

[24] Der Flieger" – Yearbook of the German Aviation Association, 1913, p. 58.

[25] Adolf Galland, whose book "The First and the Last" is highly recommended.

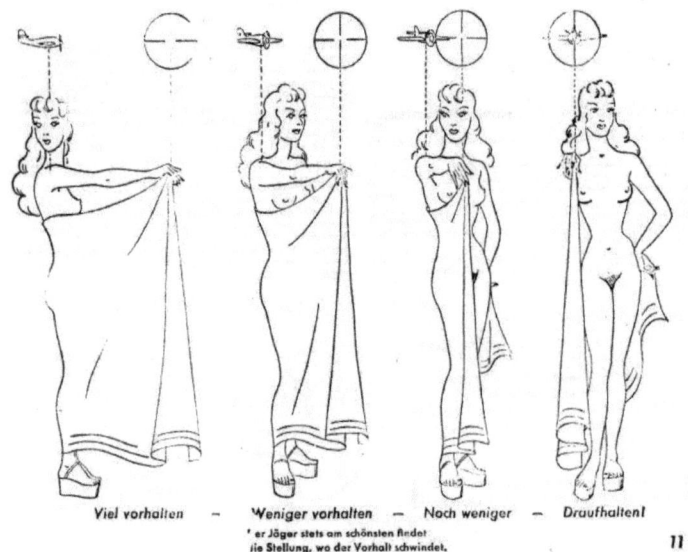

Viel vorhalten — Weniger vorhalten — Noch weniger — Draufhalten!

' er Jäger stets am schönsten findet
iie Stellung, wo der Vorhalt schwindet.

11

Visual representations of "attack angles" from the Luftwaffe
shooting manual, 1944.

Apparently, the instructions were "TOP SECRET." The Luftwaffe
didn't want their opponents to improve their own skills by
studying the German methods of distance estimation, which were
illustrated in.

Bom Dia – Beja

From 1963 to 1993, a detachment of the German Air Force were stationed in Beja, Portugal.

According to a joint governmental agreement, the airfield was designated as a rear base for aircraft maintenance and as a depot for German combat aircraft, specifically the F-104G at the time. Following initial infrastructure expansion at "Base-11", a residential complex with around 330 apartments was built on the southwestern outskirts of Beja for the German soldiers and their families.

At the center of the 4-ship formation over Beja was the German Quarter.

With the NATO strategy shift from "Massive Retaliation" to "Flexible Response," the original purpose of the German base became obsolete. Starting in 1970, the airfield served as a training base for Luftwaffe jet squadrons, enabling intensive low-altitude flying exercises and the use of the Alcochete Air-to-Ground Range near Lisbon three days a week. The ideal weather in Portugal's hottest and sunniest region guaranteed effective training sessions.

In southern Portugal, the minimum altitude for low-level flights was 250 feet, while night flights required an altitude of 500 feet.

Beginning in 1980, the Luftwaffe expanded its use of the airfield by establishing a permanent command with dedicated aircraft. In addition to regular deployments of F-104G and F-4F/RF-4E squadrons, a permanent training squadron for Alpha Jet flight training was established. Eighteen Alpha Jets were permanently stationed at Beja, and in the event of a defense scenario, they would have been assigned to Fighter Bomber Wing (JaboG) 44 in Leipheim.

Me, at daily operational planning as Operations Officer.

Pilots from Fighter Bomber Wings 41, 43, and 49 were deployed to Beja for one or two weeks at a time. Additionally, tactical low-level flight training and gunnery training for prospective Alpha Jet pilots and Tornado crews as part of the Tornado Lead-In Program

176

were conducted there. This program provided foundational tactical training between completing of the US pilot training and transitioning to the Tornado weapons system.

Return flight from Alcochete Range. A training weapon pod is visible under the right wing.

Back in the parking position in front of the main maintenance hangar in Beja, Portugal.

In the 1980s, the core staff included nine flight instructors, including the Commander, S-3 Officer, Squadron Leader, and Operations Officer. Including maintenance and support personnel, general services, and administration, up to 250 soldiers, civil servants, and their families were stationed in Beja.

The sparsely populated southern region of Portugal, combined with the optimal infrastructure, the housing provided for German families, and the friendly relationship between the Portuguese population and the soldier's families, contributed to a fulfilling and memorable time for those stationed there. Many former personnel developed a strong affinity for Portugal that remains to this day.

Attack on private vehicles belonging to German soldiers in Beja. Several explosives detonated under vehicles.

However, there were political activists who violently opposed the presence of the Luftwaffe. In February 1985, the terrorist organization FP-25 ("Forças Populares 25 de Abril") carried out a bomb attack on the private vehicles of German soldiers in the

"Bairro Alemão" in Beja. To the best of my knowledge, the perpetrators were never identified.

One consequence of the attacks was that German soldiers were issued "black" local license plates for their private vehicles instead of the previous "red" military plates. However, due to the types of vehicles and the prevalence of new cars, it was still obvious whether a car belonged to a German or a Portuguese.

3-ship Low-Level Formation in Portugal.

"In hot" at the Westcoast

My fellow pilot, let's call him "Jarro" - a nickname that would suit him well - arrived in the operations room early one Monday morning and told me:

Jarro: "I need an aircraft today, alone!"

Me: "What for?"

Jarro: "Don't ask, I just need it - for a low-level mission heading south!"

Me: "Jarro, what are you planning to do?"

Jarro glanced around to check who else might be listening, then leaned in close and whispered: *"Some German dropout in an old VW van on the West Coast near São André drove me crazy with his dog all weekend. He's been camping on the beach for weeks in that old VW van with expired plates, and his mutt is crapping all over the place. Over the*

Alpha Jet flying low at the Portuguese Westcoast.

weekend, his dog kept running across our towels and sniffing around our
kids - my youngest was completely grossed out by the smelly thing."

Me: "Alright, but you're not flying alone. It'll be a two-ship, and no nonsense."

Jarro: "Promise."

Two hours later, two Alpha Jets took off on the low-level route "Aljustrel," first heading south and then west toward Portugal's southwestern coast. Jarro 1 was the flight lead, with Jarro 2 (me) in formation. Jarro chose the Aljustrel route because it passed near the West Coast and inevitably over the beach at São André. The simulated target for the mission was a "small bridge," which in reality was just a log spanning a tidal stream on the beach, only 50 meters from the colorful VW van in question, one of the typical hippie vans of the 1980s.

Radio Communications:

Jarro 1: "Two, take spacing. Target in two miles, at your 11 o'clock."

Jarro 2: "Tally-ho target."

Jarro 1: "Lead pulling up...   lead in hot for strafe..."

Jarro 2: "Two pulling up... two in hot for strafe..."

Jarro 1: "Lead pulling up for dive-bombing... lead in hot for dive-bombing."

Jarro 2: "Two pulling up... two in hot for dive-bombing."

Jarro 1: "Lead in hot for rockets."

Jarro 2: "Two in hot for rockets."

Of course, there were no live weapons onboard; it was all simulated ground attack training. However, the gun camera recorded each run. The "Jarro flight" had five minutes of combat time to "work the bridge."

Jarro 1: "Let's leave the area."

Jarro 2: "Roger, two closing up into route formation."
Then Jarro whispered into his microphone: "Now I feel better."

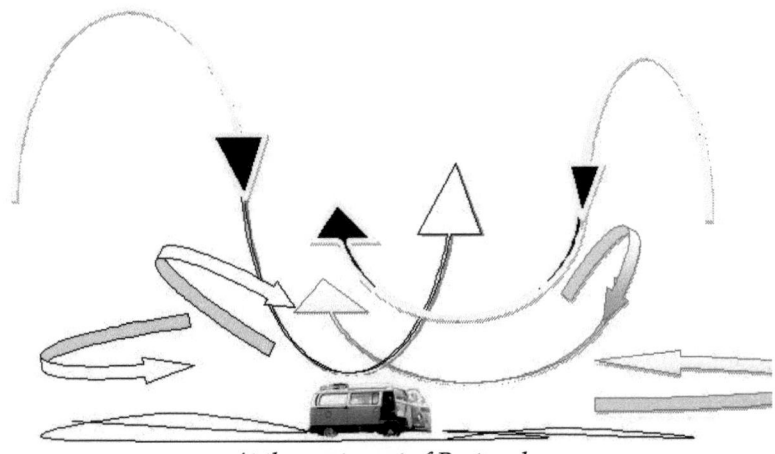

At the west coast of Portugal.

The VW van was gone from the beach the very next day and was never seen again along the Westcoast.

34 years later, I still vividly remember that flight, and I'm sure Jarro does, too. I recently read a book about the experiences of a young aviator in the early days of military aviation. The author described his squadron commander:

"Captain Ladewig could be as cheerful and youthful at the officers mess as a young lieutenant. He rarely flew himself, but when he did, it was always early in the morning. He called it 'clearing the head'. His personal aircraft was an older biplane. He would fly very low - just above the trees and hangars - in sharp turns and steep dives. If he spotted a young girl walking along the road, he would dive toward her, appearing to attack.

Later, he would laugh heartily if the startled girl raised her arms in fright to ward off the great predator or clutched her chest in panic as though to shield herself, before the mighty eagle with the uncanny roar."[26]

[26]   Friedrich Wilhelm Radenbach, Weit im Rücken des Feindes, S.25. Erinnerungen aus dem Fliegerpark Montmédy im Februar 1917.

Konya

F-100C, 54-2089, ex-USAF
131.Filo, 3.AJÜ-Konya
Geliş/arrival: 20.03.1973

Brindisi, the picturesque Italian port city, lay within sight of the eponymous Italian Air Force Base. At 7:30 am on an "Italian Wednesday morning", I stood at the counter of the military flight operations office, ready to file my flight plan from Brindisi to Konya in Turkey.

"Anybody here?" I called toward the back room, which was out of view. No one from operations was visible.

"Hello, Buon giorno," I called again, a bit louder.
Finally, a groggy Italian Sergeant appeared slowly, dressed in uniform pants, socks but no shoes, and a sleeveless undershirt, looking thoroughly sleep-deprived.

"Buon giorno, Senior Capitano," he greeted me, but his body language screamed disinterest.

"I want to file a flight plan to Turkey," I informed him politely.
"Athena Radar will be on strike from 08:00," the Sergeant replied.

That left 25 minutes before the strike began, and I hadn't yet filed the flight plan.

"OK, hurry up now, please. We'll take off in 20 minutes and be airborne by 08:00," I said firmly.

I quickly ran to the door, shouting to my fellow pilot, who was about 30 meters away: "Get the planes ready! Get in! We need to go immediately. The Greek strike starts at 08:00. If we're still on the ground, the Italians won't let us take off."

Back at the counter, I filled out the flight plan in two minutes, likely taking some liberties with the details, knowing we'd have to improvise anyway.

"You need weather information?" asked the Sergeant.

"No, grazie. Il tempo è bello," I replied, using what little Italian I knew.

Running across the tarmac, I pulled on my life vest and climbed into the rear cockpit. My pilot had just settled into the front cockpit.

"OK, start it up!" I shouted before putting on my helmet and locking the canopy.

The starter for the left engine was already spinning. Once the second engine was running, my pilot released the brakes and began taxiing. I requested taxi clearance from the tower, and the reply was stern: "You have to be airborne by 08:00, or your takeoff will be canceled."

"Roger."

"Fortuna 2, take the left side. Formation takeoff."

"Roger," responded our wingman.

At the runway threshold, we received our clearance:

"Fortuna cleared for takeoff, headwind 5 knots, contact Brindisi Radar on 276.50."

I glanced at the cockpit clock on the left instrument panel. It was two minutes to 08:00.

We rolled onto the right half of the runway, with Fortuna 2 taking the left side. I watched as my front-seat pilot pushed the throttles forward, glanced at our wingman, and nodded to confirm everything was set.

"Here we go," I said to him as I checked the instruments one last time. Everything was perfect.

His head nodded, and he released the brakes. The aircraft began rolling, the clock showing one minute to 08:00.

The runway at Brindisi ends abruptly with the Mediterranean.

As the speed indicator climbed past 80 knots, I felt the control stick begin to pull back. At 100, 120, and then 130 knots, the Alpha Jet should have lifted off - but it didn't. Ahead, I could see the runway end rapidly approaching, with only the sea beyond it.

At 140 knots, with the nose unusually high and the main landing gear still on the ground, I glanced at the flap indicator. It read: "UP."

"B., the flaps!" I shouted urgently.[27]

"You handle it - I can't," came the reply from the front cockpit.
It had been a long night at an Italian Bar!

I lowered the flaps to takeoff position, and the Alpha Jet shot into the sky like an elevator. The fence and narrow coastal strip of rock blurred beneath us before we were safely over the water, following our departure route.

"Brindisi Radar, Fortuna passing 1,000 feet, direct Kerkira."
"Fortuna, this is Brindisi Radar, loud and clear. Cleared to FL240, squawk 3120, contact Athena Radar. Goodbye."

---

[27]   Never interfere with a pilot on the controls.

186

I dialed Athena Radar's frequency into the rear radio and checked in. B. continued climbing to our assigned altitude of FL240 (24,000 feet), the TACAN needle guiding us toward Kerkira.

Then came one of the most unusual instructions of my flying career:

"Fortuna, this is Athena Radar, Kalimera. We are on strike as of 08:00. You may fly wherever you wish. Have a nice trip."

We continued toward Turkey, watching aircraft crisscross our path. During the strike, every plane seemed to fly as it pleased, within reason. Most adhered to their flight plans and assigned altitudes, as we did.

Climbing from FL260 to FL330 to save fuel, we passed a four-engine aircraft above us at FL300. It was a Boeing 747 from Emirates Airways. We maintained FL330 until entering Turkish airspace, where "free flying" ended, and Izmir Radar guided us toward Konya.

Seeing the airfield ahead, as shown in the photo, we ended our radar-guided flight, contacted Konya Tower, and landed under visual flight rules. It was the shortest and fastest route to conserve fuel, which was now dangerously low. While sufficient for landing, it wouldn't have allowed a diversion.

A Night at Brindisi.

The House!, oder "Antalya'nın genelev"

We only stayed one night in Konya before taking an Intercity Bus to Antalya to spend the weekend at the Turkish coast. The Commander of Konya airfield had informed us, that a vehicle would be made available for us in Antalya and that we should enjoy the next few days in Turkey.

Major Yildrim met us at the Bus Station in Antalya. He was standing by his black service limousine, dressed in the blue uniform of a Turkish Air Force officer. We noticed he didn't wear a pilot's badge on his chest, so it was clear he wasn't a pilot. It seemed he had been ordered to host us for the weekend. Whether the purpose was to entertain us, monitor us, or ensure nothing happened that could cause military trouble, we didn't know, nor did we care much. At the very least, we had a "chauffeur" with the rank of a Turkish Major, access to an official vehicle, and a translator, although his English, as we later discovered, was only marginally better than our Turkish. Still, his Turkish was undoubtedly excellent, or so we assumed. Moreover, he was a figure of authority, a fact that would become evident over the next 48 hours.

He dropped us off at a pleasant hotel and promised to wait outside at 7:00 pm to take us to dinner. He was in time.

"Come with me," he told us, and we followed him to his car. However, his vehicle was no longer the sleek black limousine, it was now an old Renault.

"Is that your private car?" asked my companion, seated on the worn-out passenger seat.

"Yes, my car."

"We're going to a nice restaurant. They have good food."

"That's great," I replied.

He took us to an excellent restaurant located in the citadel of Antalya. I still remember him greeting the restaurant owner, an old

188

lady, with a hand kiss, a sign of respect that highlighted her prominent societal status.

We drank Turkish red wine, and Yildrim immediately ordered a bottle of "Raki". His first glass consisted of two fingers of "Raki", topped with five fingers of water. By 11:00 pm, his last glass was five fingers of "Raki" with just two fingers of water.

When we left the restaurant, Yildrim was drunk. He struggled visibly to unlock the driver's door. Once all four of us were back in the Renault, he opened the glove compartment, searching for something. Out tumbled a pistol, landing between my companion's legs. It looked like a 6.35 mm caliber, but perhaps a 9mm. Yildrim retrieved it from between my friend's thighs, shoved it back into the glove compartment, and slammed it shut. Then, starting the engine, he said:

"We go to the house."

"To our hotel?"

"No, to the house," he replied, his speech slurred.

"Which house?" I asked.

"The house. You will see," he muttered before driving off.

We asked whether we were going to his home or perhaps a nightclub.

"You will see. We go to the house."

We were a bit tense. First, our driver was drunk. Second, he was an officer. Third, we had no idea where this journey was taking us as we left the city center of Antalya.

A few kilometers from the city, he turned onto a dark road lined with trees but not quite an avenue. I can't even recall if it was paved or a dirt road. After a few minutes, we saw a cluster of sparsely lit houses, resembling the small villages in rural areas in the 1960s. Five houses, a tavern, two streetlamps.

I noticed many parked cars along the road. People moved between the cars, some heading toward the houses, others returning. Yildrim reversed into a parking spot with surprising precision, despite his intoxication.

"Let's go. We are here," he said.

We got out of the Renault, without the pistol, which I hoped was still in the glove compartment, and followed Major Yildrim to an entrance. At a small metal table sat a policeman checking everyone entering through a gated door leading to the houses. We didn't need to show our ID; our escort explained who we were in Turkish, and we were allowed through. I now noticed that the area was enclosed by a fence. Inside, men strolled along dusty paths past the houses, stopping occasionally, chatting, or doubling back.

"Good heavens, it's a brothel," I realized.

Yildrim's "The house" turned out to be Antalya's red-light district. It became clear that our "translator" didn't know words like "brothel" in English, so he simply called it "The House."

Yildrim showed us around the "houses," which were more like shacks resembling chicken coops on farms. Four or five women lived in each "house", and there were about ten in total. Each shack had its door wide open, allowing men to size up the women,

Turkish Brothel in Antalya.

which we did as well. Men would choose their preference a process I abstained from.

As the night grew cooler, the "traffic" in and around the houses continued. We estimated activity based on the number of men entering and exiting the shacks.

Yildrim took us to "House Number One".

"You pay here," he explained.

We watched as men handed Turkish Lira to a "crumpled old woman" in exchange for chips. There were red, yellow, blue, and green chips, perhaps others for VIPs.

"Should we?" my companion asked.

"Not me," I replied firmly. I wasn't going to partake, even if it offended Yildrim.

In Turkey, visiting a brothel was often a rite of passage for young men or a group outing among friends, neighbors or colleagues. We observed animated discussions among the men, likely debating the merits of various women, as they might at home about football matches featuring Galatasaray Istanbul.

The women, dressed in bikinis, waited by wood-burning stoves, displaying themselves to potential clients.

"I like the blonde one; I think I'll pick her," said the pilot from our second aircraft, who had flown as "Fortuna 2" to Konya. Looking past ten or fifteen men, I gave my "expert assessment."

"Good figure," I said.

"Hopefully, she still has teeth," I added sarcastically.

Yildrim accompanied my friend to "House Number One" to purchase a yellow chip for the blonde Turkish woman. I trailed them back to the shack, observing the transaction.

"What now?" my friend asked, looking at us.

"Now you show her the chip, and she'll take you," I guessed.

At that moment, we saw another man hand her a yellow chip, after which she disappeared behind one of three doors in the shack.

We stood outside observing the men around us spinning their chips in their fingers, yellow, red, and green tokens glinting under the dim lights.

"You're number eight," I said. "Good luck!"

Our companion never redeemed his yellow chip. Instead, he kept it as a marker for card games back home.

On Monday we flew back to Germany via Brindisi and never mentioned the evening again.

Fighter Pilots Parties

In all NATO Air Forces it was customary not only to train aerial combat together and against each other but also to celebrate together sometimes quite enthusiastically. The days were demanding in the cockpit, and the evenings were filled with camaraderie at the bar.[28] Despite the lively celebrations in the evenings, intensive flying took place during the day.

"Squadron partnerships" developed special friendships between squadrons of allied Air Forces. One example of an exceptionally close relationship was between the 1st Fighter Bomber Squadron of JaboG 49 and the No. II Squadron[29] of the Royal Air Force. Occasional visits from delegations were followed by return visits, often linked to traditional regional events. For instance, regular visits during "Oktoberfest" were popular since Munich was practically on our doorstep.

During my time stationed in Beja, Portugal, the German instructor pilots maintained close ties with our Portuguese Air Force counterparts. Visits to their home airfields and informal exchanges over coffee or, in Portugal, over a cup of "Bica" (a strong espresso) were common.

Once a year we gathered in Beja for a joint pilot party, the "shockwaves" of which were off the charts on the "party scale." Sometimes things got quite wild. However, these parties never ended without fireworks or explosive devices, though serious injuries were thankfully avoided.

Games and competitions were a tradition that we upheld. The evening always began with a formal dinner, polite exchanges, and the presentation of gifts before someone inevitably called out "Dead Buck." This meant that whoever was the last person seated while everyone else lay flat on the floor like a "dead bug" would

---

28   Recommended reading: "The Great Santini" by Pat Conroy.

29   No. 2 Squadron RAF

have to buy the next round. The rule was absolute, applying to everyone, from the youngest Lieutenant to the oldest Colonel.

"Dead Buck" was a "higher command" that had to be obeyed.

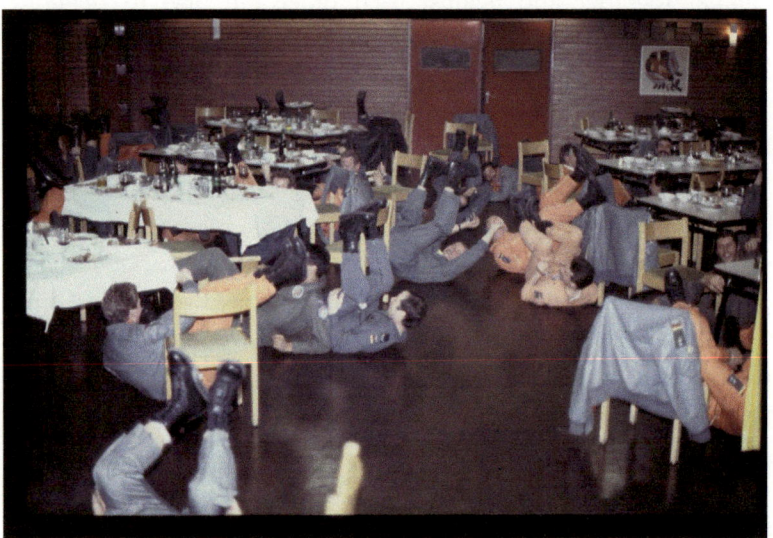

"Dead Buck" in the Officers' Mess (1986)

Once the "offender" was identified, everyone sorted out their legs, and any broken glass was swept away to avoid injuries during the next round of "Dead Buck". The dinner then resumed.

As the evening progressed, it could spiral into a "Game Without Borders"[30], though this wasn't mandatory. Some pilots were not only passionate flyers but also enthusiastic pyrotechnicians. A Portuguese party without fireworks or explosives was unthinkable. As for what the donkey might have had used for,[31] I can't recall,

---

[30]   Recommended viewing: "The Great Santini." The opening scene portrays an authentic pilot party.

[31]   Apologies - I wasn't responsible for the idea; I merely took the photo.

though I assume it was some kind of alcohol. In 1987, in some countries, a donkey was - after all - just a donkey.

"The mascot always joined us at the bar..."

One popular game was the "taxi exercise," where the pedal controls were reversed. This test revealed who still had coordination skills after five Portuguese brandies.

In the 1970s and 1980s, imagination

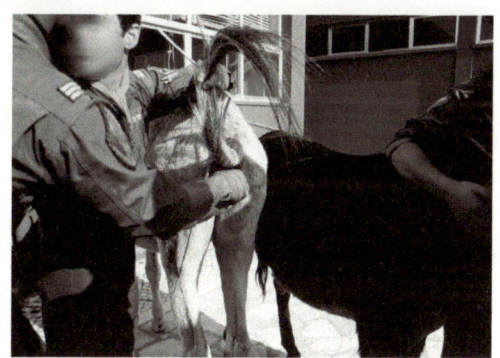

No party without the donkey.

knew no bounds so long as no one got hurt.

Various games to entertain and amuse were a well-established tradition in Air Forces and worth preserving. Even in the early days of military aviation, they were part of the social life in pilots messes. Guests, like officers from the army, often watched the pilots' antics with disbelief or even horror.

Obstacle course with reversed controls: press right steer left.

A pilot from the "60th Squadron" once recounted stories of his squadron mate "Billy" Bishop, a Canadian flying ace with 72 victories in 1917:

He described Bishop as a sort of "Prima Donna" and a "universally popular comrade known for his habit of attaching the garters and stockings of his French girlfriends to his plane's landing gear and for the exuberance with which he threw himself into the most outrageous party games."[32]

---

[32] No Empty Chairs von Ian Mackersey, Page 214

Ejectionseat Training

In 1986, the pyrotechnicians struck again in "Monte Real". A metal canister was turned upside down and placed on a stone block, with a charge of black powder placed inside.

A trail of black powder was laid from the outside to beneath the canister and then ignited. Neither the explosive force nor the time until ignition could be predicted. Despite this unpredictability, there were never any serious injuries.

For the truly daring, there was an escalation: the "Night Shot" with blindfolds. As shown in the photos, we kept a considerable distance from the "delinquent", as small stones, sand, and dust flew several meters in all directions.

197

No "Pilot's Party" without pyrotechnics!

"Knight games" with blindfolds in "Monte Real" 1987.

Gunpowder smoke at the Bar .

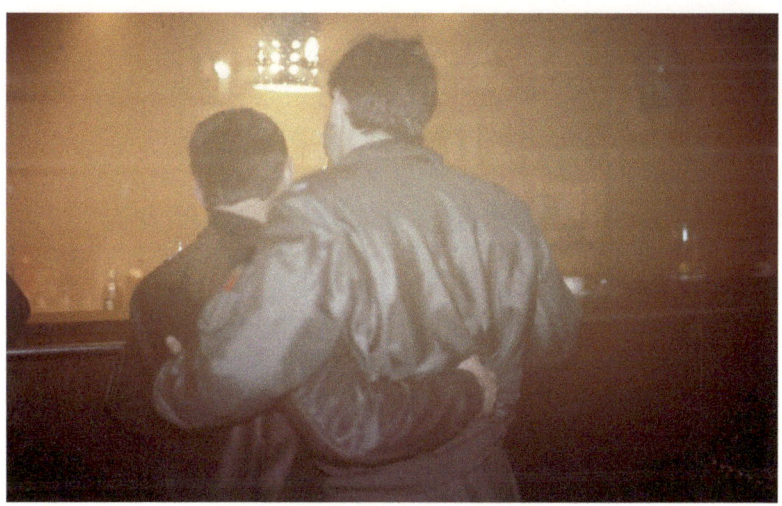

Appeasement after the "Battle".

Coin Check

When a pilot called a "Coin Check" at the Bar, all aviators, pilots and WSOs, had only 15 seconds to display their coin. Anyone without a coin, or the last to produce theirs, had to buy the next round of drinks. Conversely, if every aviator presented their coin within the allotted time, the person who initiated the "Coin Check" was required to order drinks for everyone present. This challenge was particularly popular among U.S. pilots.

Carrier Landing

Two long tables were set up end-to-end, forming the runway of an aircraft carrier. Alongside the tables, pilots gathered to "observe" the landing. At the far end of the tables stood the "Signal Officer," who gave the landing clearance. One pilot or WSO was chosen to "land." The tables were drenched in beer to make the "runway" suitably "rain-slick."

The designated pilot took a running start, dove onto the tables, and slid across the surface, aiming to stop just short of the "runway's edge". If they were too fast, they "fell into the sea" at the end of the tables.

A few beers beforehand significantly reduced any hesitation about attempting the "carrier landing."

After about eight beers, participants were ready for the next level: a nighttime landing with blindfolds on the table. However, the risk of injury rose exponentially with the blood alcohol level.

At the "British Club" in Decimommanu, Sardinia, "Carrier Landings" often became the event of choice after midnight.

In the U.S. Navy, "Carrier Landings" were infamous, as was the notorious "Gauntlet" held on the third floor of the Hilton Hotel in Las Vegas.

On September 5, 1991, the U.S. Navy faced a significant scandal during the "Tailhook" convention. According to an investigative report, more than 4,000 men and women participated in the event.

The fallout from the 1991 Tailhook Party ultimately had severe consequences for the careers of fourteen admirals and nearly three hundred U.S. Navy pilots.[33]

For more on fighter pilot traditions, check out the book by former fighter pilot Rob Burgon: "Piano Burning and Other Fighter Pilot Traditions."[34]

The Airman's Lament

> I am an aviator, I will not drink,
> But if I do, I will not get drunk,
> But if I do, I will not stagger,
> But if I do, I will not fall down,
> But if I do, I will fall Face First,
> so No one Can See "My Wings".

Colonel C.R. Anderegg of the USAF described it in his own words:

"The mainstay of social live was the officer's club, and alcohol use was the linchpin of camaraderie after duty hours. Fighter pilots have always loved

---

[33]   The Mother of All Hooks: Story of the U.S.Navy's Tailhooks Scandal: The Story of the U.S. Navy's Tailhook, by William H. McMichael.

[34]   See: „Piano Burning and Other Fighter Pilot Traditions".

games and competition, especially drinking games, and the officer's club environment provided the perfect venue for both. All clubs hat a stag bar where women were forbidden to enter, and penalty for even a telephone call from a wife was a free round of drinks for by the chagrined husband.

Many commanders attempted to dam some games, not because they were stupid, but because injuries caused disruption in the flying schedule and if an injured Player had to be replaced the next morning. Flying hard and drinking hard were expected among the peers of the fighter squadron. Those who did not do both were suspect, and those who did were expected to be perfect the next day on the mission, following a Fighter Pilot's breakfast, a Coke, a candy bar, and a cigarette."[35]

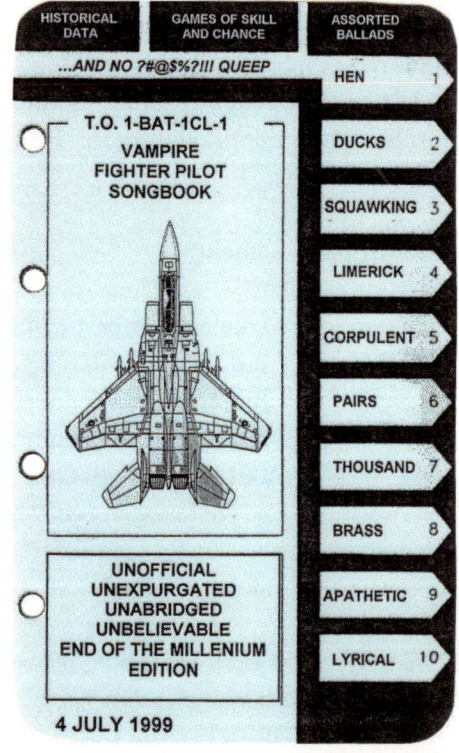

---

[35]   Colonel C.R. Anderegg USAF, Sierra Hotel S.50.

Weapons Instructor Course

The highest qualification a fighter pilot could achieve was becoming a weapons instructor.

In the 1970s, 80s, and 90s, the hierarchy of qualifications for fighter pilots in an operational squadron placed the squadron pilots, nicknamed "line pigs," at the bottom of the food chain. Next came the flight section leaders, followed by the flight instructors, and at the very top were the weapons instructors. The weapons instructors were the true experts in tactics and weapon deployment. Those chosen for this elite role were meticulously selected. In the F-104G and F-4 communities, weapons instructors were distinguished by their "patch" (target-arm), which for some pilots held more prestige than their pilot badge.

In addition to this pinnacle of combat pilot qualifications, there were roles like the maintenance flight certification, for conducting technical check-flights following significant work on an aircraft, such as an engine replacement. There were also "Aircraft Inspection Officers" (LÜBs), who were essentially "light flight instructors" authorized to conduct annual checks for instrument flight certification, the "60-4 Check," or the Combat Ready Check for the "Line Pigs." Furthermore, there were "standardizers," responsible for ensuring and evolving standardized flying procedures.

The weapons instructor training for Alpha Jet pilots took place at FBW 49 in Fürstenfeldbruck. This was the home base for weapons instructors in the "Tactical Training and Experimental Group". The curriculum was rigorous, encompassing the technical aspects of Alpha Jet weaponry and all the armaments deployable by the Alpha Jet, including the onboard cannon, BL755 cluster bombs, unguided rockets, 250 kg unretarded bombs (HDGP), MK82 retarded bombs, N-Containers (Napalm), "chaff and flares," and the ECM Jammer.

Weapons effects calculations, tactical formations, and mission planning were demanding. Avoiding interception by enemy fighters while completing the bombing mission was a constant challenge, requiring both skill and airborne leadership qualities.

The academic training took place in Fürstenfeldbruck, as did some of the aerial weaponry exercises, without the involvement of "enemy fighters." The large-scale missions, including F-4F Phantoms interceptors, were conducted in Beja, Portugal. For specific missions, such as a "massive air attack" on a Portuguese airfield, we were supported by Portuguese A-6P aircraft acting as interceptors. Anti-helicopter training missions were flown from FBW 43 in Oldenburg, with UH-1D and CH-53 helicopters simulating enemy targets. These were perilous low-speed flights at extremely low altitudes, often at the lower limits of the Alpha Jet's flying speed.

A critical aspect of the training was pushing the operational envelope of the weapon system and extending personal limits. Graduates returned to their squadrons as weapons instructors and "multipliers," improving tactical effectiveness in daily training.

An Example Training Mission:
Airfield attack on Tancos airfield. "Mustang 1" led the formation for a planned attack on Tancos airfield (LPTN). The "frag-order," or detailed mission order, outlined the roles: Four aircraft equipped with MK 82 LDGB 500-pound bombs (227 kg) would target stationary objectives, while four others carrying CBU bombs would temporarily disable airfield operations.

The MK 82 fuses were set to a tenth-of-a-second delay, allowing the bombs to penetrate the concrete before detonating, causing craters that would render the airfield temporarily unusable. The CBUs were intended to destroy soft targets like aircraft and vehicles, or at least render them inoperable. Each BL-755 dispersed 147 bomblets, with each capable of disabling a vehicle.

The aircraft were prepped the evening before, and technical checks were completed. During the weapons instructor course, airfield attack exercises used inert weapons for training. Live ordnance was reserved for designated air-to-ground ranges, unavailable in Portugal.

The mission briefing included a thorough review of enemy air threats, emphasizing the heavily defended nature of enemy airfields. Surface-to-air missiles (SAMs) like the SA-6, SA-8, and SA-9, as well as anti-aircraft artillery (AAA) such as the ZSU 23-2 and the feared ZSU 23-4, posed significant risks. The ZSU 23-4, for instance, could fire a devastating barrage of 200 rounds per barrel per minute.

The attack required a precise, well-coordinated "one pass, haul ass" approach.

Execution of the Mission:

Taking off from Beja Air Base, "Mustang Lead" led the formation toward "Alpha North," a reservoir near the airfield. Maintaining 95% throttle allowed the following sections to catch up and form a cohesive formation. Ten minutes ahead, two F-4Fs were tasked with clearing the route and engaging any enemy fighters.

In the low-altitude combat air patrol (Low-CAP), the F-4Fs disrupted enemy radar operations, giving the bombers a better chance of reaching their target.

The Mustang formation maintained a tactical "Card Four Formation" for mutual protection and early warning against interceptors. The mission demanded tight timing and coordination, particularly during the final approach to the target.

At the initial point (IP), the flight pushed their throttles to 95%, accelerating to 400 knots. Within moments, the formation began their attack runs. Each pilot carefully aligned their bombing equipment and weapons settings, concentrating on the task at hand.

As "Mustang Lead" pulled up for the first attack, the remaining formations followed with precise spacing to avoid overlap or collision. Each wave of simulated bomb drops was evaluated afterward using the gun camera footage.

Following the attack, the flight reassembled in tactical formation, reducing speed to conserve fuel, and returned to Beja Air Base.

The training underscored the complexity and intensity of airfield attacks, highlighting the critical importance of planning, precision, and teamwork in combat operations.

Mixed Alpha Jet and F-4F Phantom Formation.

Bird Strike

Both engines ran smoothly, the throttles set to 88%, propelling our jet at 360 knots, approximately 660 km/h. The town of Pöttmes was behind us, and we were flying on a course of 324° to our next waypoint. Our altitude was 500 feet above ground, the standard low-level altitude in Germany.

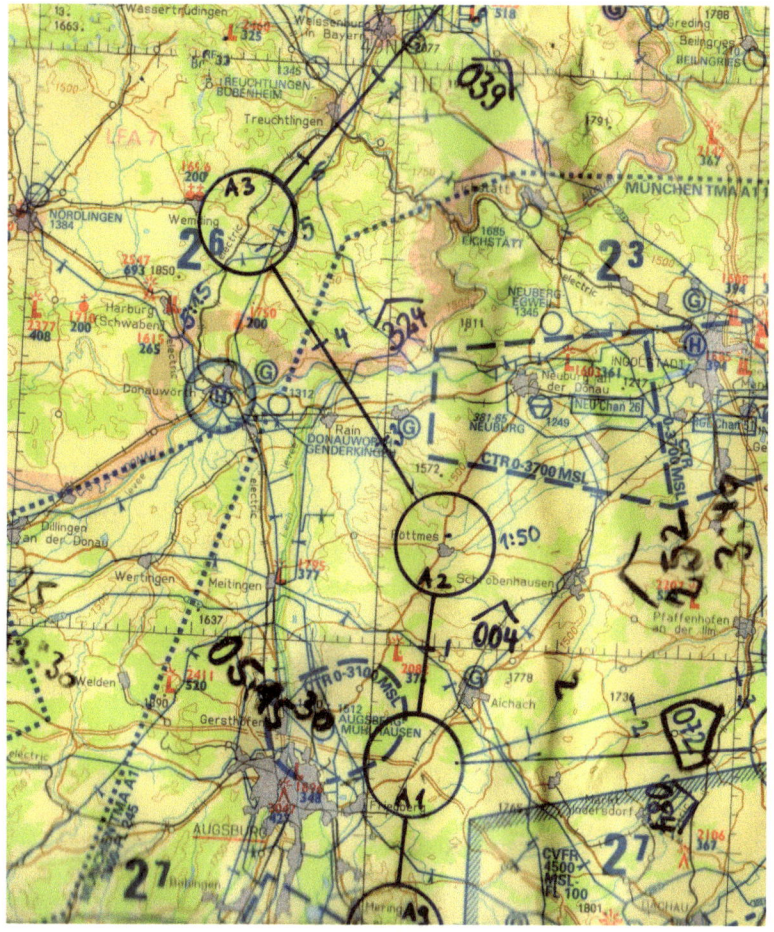

Low Level Map.

In the front cockpit was Lieutenant Colonel K., while I sat in the rear as a flight instructor. This wasn't a typical training flight. I was assigned to fly with Lieutenant Colonel K. because he was classified as a "currency holder," someone who logged only 70 flight hours annually due to a primary posting in the ministry. After extended breaks from flying, we usually scheduled a few flights with an instructor to help currency holders regain their routine.

This allowed me to dedicate part of my attention to the summer landscape. After 3:45 minutes we crossed the Danube, passing the town of Rain on the right, a place where a supersonic boom had once shattered numerous windows. Four minutes later, Donauwörth appeared on our left, with our next waypoint, a rail-road intersection, at 5:15 minutes.

Our course was precise, speed steady at 360 knots, and altitude perfect. The radar altimeter, set to 500 feet, confirmed our altitude above ground.

From the left I saw a railroad track, and to the right of our flight path, a road exited Monheim. The intersection of the tracks and the road marked our waypoint. The next calculated course was 039°.

My arms rested on either side of the canopy, and my gaze shifted between the navigation chart in my left hand, the landscape, and occasionally, the cockpit clock. I watched the second hand tick toward the 30-second mark, the minute hand at five minutes.

"Birds!"

Both of us spotted them - 10 to 15 birds, not a large flock. I quickly shouted "Birds" into the microphone, but any reaction was already too late; the time from spotting to impact was a fraction of a second.

"Bang!" It was a sound loud enough to suggest a wing had been torn apart.

"Bird strike, we've hit a bird," came through from the front cockpit.

"Yes," I confirmed. I'd seen it coming.

Both our gazes briefly checked the engine instruments, which displayed normal readings. Lieutenant Colonel K. was an experienced pilot. I assisted by providing checklist procedures aloud for him to follow.

K. had already pitched the aircraft nose up, climbing to 5,000 feet. The climb alone reduced our speed from 360 to 250 knots without altering engine power.

At this moment we didn't know if we had hit only one bird or several birds, or whether a bird had been ingested into an engine. K. simultaneously initiated a right turn southward. Neuburg Air Base was just minutes to the east, ideal for an emergency landing. Ingolstadt and Lechfeld were also potential options west of Fürsty.

The flight controls felt normal, and the engines and hydraulics appeared intact. For all airborne emergencies, the first principles of emergency procedures applied:

1. Maintain Aircraft Control.
2. Analyze the Situation and Take Proper Action.
3. Land as Soon as Practicable.

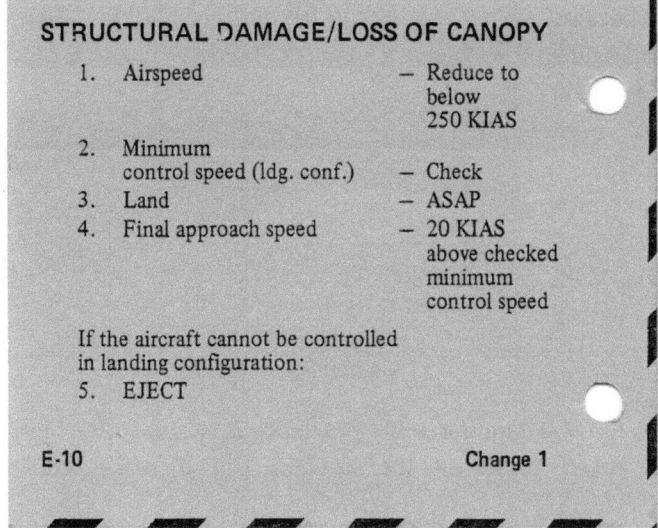

STRUCTURAL DAMAGE/LOSS OF CANOPY

1.	Airspeed	— Reduce to below 250 KIAS
2.	Minimum control speed (ldg. conf.)	— Check
3.	Land	— ASAP
4.	Final approach speed	— 20 KIAS above checked minimum control speed

If the aircraft cannot be controlled in landing configuration:

5.	EJECT	

E-10   Change 1

We climbed to a safe altitude to allow sufficient time to respond to engine or hydraulic failure, or, in the worst case, loss of aircraft control. Time was measured in seconds, but enough to react.

We followed the checklist for "Structural Damage" and prepared for an emergency landing at our home base. K. declared a bird strike emergency and requested a straight-in approach from Fürsty tower. He maintained 250 knots until we were positioned to reduce speed to 195 knots, deploy the landing gear, set flaps, and approach at 20 knots above the usual speed.

The aircraft remained responsive, but we were unsure about the extent of the damage.

During the final approach, the blue flashing lights of fire trucks became visible. We knew the flight surgeon had also been automatically alerted and was stationed mid-runway with the medical truck.

The damage at the stabilator.

K. executed the landing with practiced precision. The higher approach speed increased the landing roll distance. During landings with structural damage, a higher speed is maintained to mitigate risks of stalling due to altered aerodynamics.

The brakes functioned properly. We stopped on the runway, shutting down the engines as per procedure. Taxiing would require throttle adjustments, potentially exacerbating any engine damage from the bird strike.

A tow truck was already waiting to quickly clear the runway for the following traffic. Only then did we see that a single bird had struck the right horizontal stabilizer.

The bird strike left noticeable damage but underscored the effectiveness of emergency protocols and the importance of a composed, methodical response in-flight.

Cloud Surfing

The landing gear was retracted, and at 180 knots, I raised the flaps from "Down" to "Up," accelerating to 360 knots, the designated low-level flight speed. At an altitude of 200 feet, I entered the inversion layer predicted by our meteorologist. The world around me turned gray, void of vibrant colors. Now I had to rely solely on my instruments. Although I wasn't flying through thick clouds, the thin, gray-brown haze was dense enough to obscure the view. I knew, that within seconds I would break through this inversion layer and leave the lifeless gray mass behind.

I could already see the sun faintly, like through frosted glass. Its light grew brighter, the surroundings more vivid, until suddenly, the brilliant blue Portuguese sky appeared above me. A postcard perfect sky.

My mission was a low-level flight to northern Portugal, a self-assigned task since, as operations officer for the training squadron, I had considerable freedom in planning flights, provided they adhered to the Tactical Combat Training Program (TCTP).

I quickly climbed to the prescribed low-level altitude of 500 feet, gradually pulling the throttles back to 92% power as my speed stabilized at 360 knots.

"Fortuna, Alpha North, leaving," I reported to Beja Tower (LPBJ). "Fortuna cleared to leave, have a nice trip," replied the air traffic controller, and I switched my radio to Channel 12, the squadron's frequency.

The Odivelas reservoir lay 500 feet below me, though I couldn't see it; I knew it was there, as it was our daily departure point for low-level flights northward after exiting the control zone. Beneath me, the inversion layer stretched uninterrupted to the north, just a few meters below the fuselage of my Alpha Jet. The top of this warm air layer was as smooth as glass yet as opaque as frosted glass. My plane's shadow was invisible, cast directly below due to the close proximity of the wing surfaces to the inversion layer.

The needle of my ADF compass pointed the way, while the distance indicator showed the distance to the next waypoint. My radar altimeter, set with a warning marker at 500 feet, ensured I maintained the correct altitude. I let myself be consumed by the joy of pure flying.

The sensation of speed grew overwhelming, as the inversion layer remained constant, creating the illusion of skimming over a highway at 360 knots, just meters above the surface.

At 8 minutes and 45 seconds past the Odivelas reservoir, my navigation computer swiveled the ADF needle to a heading of 010°. I banked the jet into a 60° turn, brushing the "imaginary glass" with my wingtip, almost as if etching a line with a glass cutter.

Alpha Jet over the "Serra da Estrela".

The weather created a surreal experience I had never encountered in over 2,000 flight hours. I was intoxicated by the sense of speed and longed to prolong the exhilaration. Occasionally, the radar altimeter beeped when a hill brought the ground closer than 500 feet, only to go silent moments later as I cleared the obstacle.

I noticed on sporadic checks of the altimeter that I dipped slightly below the minimum altitude but regained height quickly

213

over valleys. True contour flying, following the terrain, was impossible under these conditions. The upper surface of the inversion layer remained mirror-smooth but impenetrable.

Eventually, the frequency of altitude warnings increased, disrupting the sacred-like mood of the flight. I adjusted the altimeter warning marker to 350 feet, reasoning that the uninhabited hills below wouldn't mind. The minimum authorized low-level altitude of 250 feet during such missions had already been cleared.

Flying just meters above the dense haze I felt drawn to gently touch its surface. Now it felt as though I was racing directly on the "highway" at 660 km/h.

As the haze thinned after several northern waypoints, my radar altimeter began warning of minor deviations below 350 feet. Determined to savor the speed, I silenced the persistent alerts, setting the marker to "0." I trusted the safety of remaining above the milky layer in this familiar and unpopulated region.

The navigation computer indicated I was approaching my final waypoint within the Peneda-Gerês National Park. Over 30 minutes into the flight, I had spent this time reveling in a euphoric sense of speed, traveling six miles per minute, one mile every ten seconds.

As I reached the next waypoint and began a 160° left turn with 4g in a smooth 60° bank, my blood froze in an instant.

Emerging from the milky soup ahead of me were the top fifteen or maybe twenty feed of a spindly tree. The inversion layer was now only a few feet thick but remained as opaque as before.

Instinctively, I yanked the stick back, narrowly avoiding the tree. Seconds later the radar altimeter read 500 feet again.

Resetting the warning marker to 500 feet, I flew the planned route back to land on runway 01L at Beja.

That moment of shock remains vividly etched in my memory, as do the exhilarating feelings of that extraordinary flight.

Suddenly, I saw a barren tree emerging from the clouds.

Low Flying Aera 7

My gaze caught an Alpha Jet engaged in a dogfight with two Phantoms, flanked by two British Jaguars and a USAF A-10. It seemed as though everyone was chasing everyone else.

A F-4F Phantom, though I couldn't tell whether it was a German F-4F, likely from Neuburg, or a U.S. F-4E Phantom from Spangdahlem, turned toward me attacking from the 7 o'clock position. I was sure the pilot intended to get within cannon firing range. Unable to speed away, and with my wingman unable to assist, I had to save my own skin. Tight turns were the Alpha Jet's best defense at low altitude to escape an opponent's line of fire.

The g-meter indicated: 5g, 5.5g, 6g. I kept the stick steady, forcing the F-4, with its speed advantage, out of my turning radius attempting to reverse the situation. I cautiously reduced my bank angle to gain altitude, altitude equals energy. But the opponent was quick, tightening his turn and re-engaging me in another close dogfight.

In the heat of the fight, I identified the "enemy" as a U.S. F-4E. I couldn't shake them; they clung to me like a magnet. It became clear that the F-4E pilot was pushing me and my Alpha Jet to its limits. As long as we spiraled around each other in tight turns, he couldn't line up for a simulated shot, but I was losing speed and couldn't maintain my turn radius or altitude. I faced a choice: enter a descent or ease off my high-g turn to avoid stalling the aircraft, a dangerous situation that could end up with falling out of the sky. I realized this battle was lost.

The opponent, seeing they were in a "Fox 3" position and only needed to pull the trigger, pulled up and disappeared above me ending the engagement.

I had lost this dogfight, at least this simulated one. I rolled beneath him, catching the antennas atop the hill of Hesselberg in my peripheral vision, and reoriented myself to locate "Fortuna 2," my wingman.

This game of cat and mouse, without live weapons, lasted only two or three minutes, but in a real combat scenario against an armed adversary, it would have felt like an eternity.

One of the F-4Es climbed steeply out of sight, while the other disappeared toward the horizon, its smoke trail barely visible. Both were likely heading back to Spangdahlem "Spang" Air Base.

Fight as you train and train as you fight.

Low Flying Area 7 – Hesselberg

I turned my thoughts away from them, chasing fighter planes wasn't my mission as a fighter-bomber, and we wouldn't stand a chance against F-4s cruising at 420 knots at low altitude.

At my 2 o'clock, I noticed two dark dots about 3-4 miles away, moving east. They were two American A-10s - potential targets of opportunity. I kept them in sight. Due to their slower speed, usually around 300 knots in low-level flight, I had a chance to approach their 6 o'clock position unnoticed. I positioned myself at a height where I could see them against the horizon while remaining below it, making my aircraft harder to spot.

As I maneuvered into a right-hand turn to trail them more closely, the dots turned into aircraft. Suddenly, they executed a sharp right turn and came toward us - they'd spotted us.

At my 4 o'clock, "Fortuna 2" held his position, ensuring we avoided any collisions.

"Fortuna 2, turn left, heading south, back to route."

"Two," he confirmed.

I kept an eye on the two A-10s, which didn't pursue us further. We steadily distanced ourselves from them. I refocused on navigation to continue our low-level route toward the planned target. My wingman advanced into his correct position, a mile to my left at 9 o'clock.

"Fortuna flight, hard right, go," came over the radio. It was my No 2 calling.

"F-15s, 5 to 6 o'clock, closing."

I was already pulling 6g in a right turn when I spotted the two F-15Cs. We were now their target of opportunity. Trapped, we could only sustain a tight turn for a short time at low altitude before losing too much speed. Climbing was not an option against fighter jets of this class; we were defenseless. Our only hope was to disrupt their setup for a shot and then escape as low as possible - and that's exactly what we did.

After a 180° turn beneath them, I saw both F-15Cs switch to a steep right-hand climb, pulling away.

"Fortuna flight, hard left, go, back to route," I instructed my No 2, redirecting us to our low-level route to continue the mission.

In "Low Flying Area 7," we were cleared to fly at 250 feet. In a real combat scenario, we would have flown at treetop level. Extreme low-level flight made it harder for hunters to lock onto us and even more difficult to engage, though not impossible.

"Low, low, low" - there was no other chance of survival during the Cold War.

It wasn't uncommon for fighters to provoke fighter-bombers into a dogfight during low-level flight. In the 70s and 80s, most American fighter pilots had two tours of duty in the Vietnam War under their belts.

As Colonel C.R. Anderegg of the USAF writes in his book "Sierra Hotel":

"Sierra Hotel" - aviation slang for "Shit Hot."

"...a captain with two combat tours in Vietnam, serving at RAF Bentwaters in the early 1970s, remembers: There was little or no effect on the part of the combat veterans to follow the rules. Each squadron had is own code of right or wrong. One example he recalls were the constant mock attacks that RAF and USAF fighters made on each other. What little air-to-air training the Phantoms did was against each other. However, their low proficiency did not stop them from jumping RAF Lightnings, Hunters, and F-4s at every opportunity.

Even though **strictly forbidden** *by USAFE (United States Air Force in Europe) rules, swirling, twirling dogfights over the North Sea with national pride at stake were common-place. Captain Jumper recalls, "We had no idea what we were doing. It was just free-for-all. Sometimes it was so dangerous it wasn't even fun. It was plain stupid."*[36]

Fight to fly,
Fly to fight,
Fight to win!

Colonel Anderegg further recounts in his book how fighter pilot tactics had evolved since the 1970s. As daily "opponents," we were welcome targets of opportunity in Low Flying Area 7, near Hesselberg.

---

[36]   Colonel C.R. Andereegg, USAF, Sierra Hotel S.49 und S.184.

"Ten years later, on my second tour of duty in Europe, I took off from Bitburg Air Base, Germany, in an F–15C with my wingman. At 500 feet I leveled off and gave him a visual signal to go to tactical Formation – line-abreast, one mile apart. We flew East fast and low, making silent comm-out turns until we reached a special piece of airspace in eastern West Germany, called 'Low Fly Area 7', where we set up a combat air patrol. Over the next thirty minutes we intercepted Fighters from the German Air Force and others from the USAF at low altitude using the F–15 radar. Most of our shots were in-the-face Sidewinders. After our patrol time was up, we flew, still at low altitude, and still silently, back to Bitburg, where I turned us onto the initial approach and called the tower for landing, the first radio call I had made since asking for takeoff clearance an hour earlier. When we got back into the squadron building, my wingman and I reviewed our videocassettes to assess every shot each of us had taken. Every one of his shots was valid; mine were nearly as good.

My wingman had less than 100 hours of fighter time. To him, it was just another day in the 525th Tactical Fighter Squadron; to me it was a revelation."

"Sierra Hotel!"

The Essence of Flying

The world outside the cockpit was once again a spectacle of light and gray clouds. Mere seconds after lifting off from the runway at Erding airfield and retracting the landing gear, we were enveloped in clouds. It was a constant alternation between dramatically torn cloud fields and pitch-black, threatening cloud masses that seemed to engulf the sky. In the cockpit of my Alpha Jet, I was part of this spectacle, both observer and actor, while remaining intensely focused on the precision of formation flying. I was flying as No 2, with the lead pilot in front of me as my reference point in the formation, though he was barely visible, swallowed by the dense clouds surrounding us.

The position light on his left wing was my only anchor, yet my body told a different story. While flying parallel to the Earth, I was overcome by an intense sensation that we were inverted, a state known as "vertigo." My sense of balance was simply wrong, and my concentration was locked in a desperate battle to resist the illusion.

Formation flying in clouds, amidst strong turbulence, in a jet is an extraordinary experience, it's a blend of technical precision, adrenaline, and the constant challenge of maintaining control and position. It is a state where physical tension, mental sharpness, and deep connection with the

Flying formation in clouds.

aircraft and fellow pilots converge.

Rain streamed along the cockpit, blurring my vision in the darkness of the clouds. My instincts urged me to roll the aircraft, to follow the sensation telling me I was upside down. But rationality - the iron law of aviation - was stronger: trust your lead aircraft and the instruments, never your senses. In such moments, the trust in your formation partner is absolute. You rely on him to execute every movement with utmost precision, just as he trusts you. You fly so close together that a single mistake could be catastrophic. The sight of the position lights, gently rising and falling in sync with the flight, provides orientation - they are the anchor in a sea of dark clouds and motion.

Our visual system is typically our primary sense for orientation. It provides information about the horizon, movement, and our position in space. However, in dense clouds or darkness, a clear visual reference point is absent. Without a visible horizon, the brain can no longer distinguish whether the aircraft is level or banked. It then relies on other orientation systems, which, however, are prone to error.

Radio communication in such flight conditions was kept to an absolute minimum. Every pilot knew that any unnecessary distraction could be fatal. Occasionally, I could feel my breath in the oxygen mask, as well as my pulse pounding in my temples. The Alpha Jet felt like an extension of my body, yet for a moment - even though I gripped the control stick and throttle more firmly than usual - I felt as though I had no influence over the natural forces acting on my aircraft.

Visibility was reduced to little more than a diffuse gray, streaked with swirling clouds. The lead aircraft was sporadically out of sight, a situation that necessitated separation from the formation. A split-second decision had to be made. The throttle was pulled back immediately, allowing a fallback of at least 100 feet, eliminating the risk of collision. Those fractions of a second without visual contact with the other aircraft heightened the tension immeasurably - especially since, in tight formation, the wingtip-to-wingtip distance is only about 3 feet. The gusts and turbulence caused both jets to sway slightly, and for a brief moment, my heart seemed to stop. The feeling of inversion intensified. I had to summon every ounce of willpower not to instinctively pull the controls in the direction that felt "right." It was like balancing on a tightrope, with nothing beneath my feet and the abyss of instinct urging me in the wrong direction.

Moving cloud structures can create the illusion that the aircraft is banking or rotating, even when it is actually flying straight and holding position almost glued to the lead aircraft's wing.

Slowly, the "soup," as we pilots call it, grew brighter, then turned almost white, like milk. The clouds began to thin. A narrow strip of the horizon emerged barely perceptible at first, then clearly defined. The blue sky, seemingly unreachable just moments before, pushed through the gray clouds. With it came the certainty that  the instruments had not deceived us, and that I had, against all instincts, overcome the illusion.

On the return flight we entered the clouds once again, and the battle between senses and instruments, between concentration and formation discipline, resumed. Changes in flight attitude and speed, for example, when deploying the landing gear, made the illusions even more torturous. A simple trick sometimes helped: I imagined the earth beneath me, aligned parallel to my aircraft. This mental imagery helped recalibrating my sensory perception.

"Vertigo" is a test. A psychological battle that humbles every pilot. It is a reminder that the sky is not just about freedom but can also be a hell inside your own mind, turning into a dangerous enemy. In those moments between light and shadow, between instinct and reason, the true art of flying is born. It lies not only in technical skill but in the ability to withstand the chaos of one's own senses and to rely on, with unwavering discipline, on the instruments that safely guide us through the clouds or the night.

In aviation, such sensory illusions can be catastrophic if pilots trust their instincts or bodily sensations instead of their instruments. The result can be a misjudgment leading to an unintentional bank or an unnoticed descent. In formation flying it can result in a midair collision.

The illusion in the clouds arises because the brain attempts to compensate for the missing visual information by relying on unreliable signals from the vestibular and proprioceptive systems. This leads to false perceptions of orientation, movement, and position. That is why it is essential for pilots to read and trust their instruments, they are the only objective means of navigating safely through such sensory deceptions.

Flying in bad weather or at night is always an experience that demands technical skill, mental strength, and emotional balance. At the same time, it is a moment that shapes you forever because it tests the limits of your abilities and makes the essence of flying - control, precision, and trust - tangible in its purest form.

Lightning Stroke

Nearly three hours of flight time were behind me. With just twenty-five minutes left before I would touch down at Fürstenfeldbruck airfield (EDSF), my destination after departing Portugal. The weather forecast was autumnal stormy but sufficient for the planned landing.

At 30,000 feet the sun was still shining, as it had for most of the route. The Pyrenees had been cloudless. I had enjoyed views of the Bay of Biscay and, occasionally, the rivers and hills of France's Massif Central. Now, however, I was flying above a dense cloud layer. The weather front began as I crossed into Germany near Colmar. West of the city of Ulm, air traffic control cleared me to proceed directly to the Fürstenfeldbruck military airfield. I reduced the throttle to 80%, lowered the nose 5 degrees on the artificial horizon, and began my descent. At 28,000 feet, the clouds swallowed me; it grew darker and more turbulent. I asked ground control for the current weather update and was advised of "embedded thunderstorms" - thunderstorms hidden within the cloud layers.

"You are cleared to circumnavigate the thunderstorms," Munich Radar informed me.

How was I supposed to circumnavigate thunderstorms without onboard weather radar? The air traffic controller probably hadn't considered that, if they even knew. To make matters worse, I was running low on fuel. The flight had already taken fifteen minutes longer than planned, and it was nearing the usual closing time for the airfield. While air traffic control would likely keep the airfield open for me, there would have to be a good reason. Given the weather conditions, I had no option but to land at Fürsty. Diverting to another airfield with more reasonable weather was no longer possible.

I continued my approach. The TACAN navigation instrument needle pointed directly to the runway, and I descended to the prescribed altitude. The flashes of lightning west of Augsburg became more frequent, visible out of the corner of my eye, flickering below and beside the aircraft. Then several bolts struck simultaneously, their diffuse light obscured by dark clouds. One would have to be either naive or insane to voluntarily fly an Alpha Jet into the heart of a thunderstorm. Yet many pilots before me had similar thoughts and still had no other choice. It was often the only way to reach the safety of a runway with the fuel available.

Reports in our flight safety magazine had described other pilots' experiences flying through storms: "The aircraft's controls can fail completely. Speed indicators become entirely unreliable, with readings jumping between 50 knots and 250 knots, yet the pilot must press on through the storm's core to reach calmer air."

Flight manuals provided these scenarios in well-crafted sentences but failed to convey the brutal reality of losing control mid-storm.

The air around me trembled violently. My aircraft shook and jolted so intensely that it was sometimes impossible to read the instruments. I gripped the stick tightly with my right hand, my fingers cramping under the glove. The strain in my hands was palpable.

In a split second, the cockpit lit up like a fireball, accompanied by a deafening crack. "Bang!" It was loud and piercing, as if the aircraft were being torn apart. A lightning bolt had struck my Alpha Jet, but I didn't know where.

"Ejecting now would probably be certain death," I thought. The only option was to keep flying, trusting the principle of the Faraday cage. Just stay on course and head for the runway. The engines were running at 80%. I corrected for the turbulence as best as I could and aimed to maintain a 10-degree descent on the artificial horizon.

I pressed on. The TACAN display showed the distance I still had to endure. Twenty-two miles. I followed the compass needle... twenty miles.

As the airfield approach radar identified me, the radar approach control took over navigation, correcting my glide path. Closer and closer, I continued the course gliding toward the saving runway. The air began to calm; I seemed to have passed through the thunderstorm's core. Out of the corner of my eye, I still couldn't see the ground. The altimeter read 300 feet... 250 feet... 200 feet. The "decision height" had been reached - this was the point at which the runway should be visible.

"Fortuna, passing decision height. Runway should be in sight."

I simply replied, "Roger," avoided confirming no sight of the runway, and continued flying, bending the rules. I couldn't see the runway and didn't have enough fuel or time to divert. My eyes darted between the instruments and the windshield.

Descending further... 180 feet... 150 feet. Seconds felt like an eternity. Then, in the gray rain clouds, I spotted the approach lights - flashing beacons racing toward the runway.

I knew that after the last light came the tarmac. That's where I had to be. That's where I would land.

EDSF to EDSF

In the "good old days," there were flying opportunities that, I suspect, would be unthinkable 35 years later. In June 1983, we experienced one such "goody," as we called it back then.

In "Fürsty," the runway was scheduled for maintenance, requiring the airfield to close for flight operations. Relocating pilots and aircraft to another base would have likely been too complex, though we weren't privy to the exact reasoning of squadron leadership.

We were given the "offer" to spend five days with one of our Alpha Jets flying wherever we wanted to accumulate flight hours. We were permitted to land at any military airfield in Europe, provided we obtained landing clearance. After the last flight of the day, we were required to call our ops operations center to report our location and the destination of our next flight the following day.

One of my squadron mates and I immediately brainstormed which airfields would make for an interesting week and started planning a "grand tour" of Europe with two Alpha Jets. We got along splendidly and had already undertaken some "exciting" flights to other countries together.

On June 22, at 7:55 am, we released the brakes. Our first flight was a low-level sortie with a planned target near the city of Vechta and a landing in Oldenburg (EDNO) the home base of the FBW 43. From Oldenburg, our next low-level flight took us to Husum (EDNH), the home base of FBW 41, for a quick refuel before continuing to Strasbourg (LFST) in France. By 2:55 pm, we had landed Strasbourg, leaving us plenty of time to explore the city center and enjoy a leisurely dinner opposite the cathedral.

The requirement was to complete at least one flight each day. The following day, we planned to take off from Strasbourg at 3:10 pm and land in Valencia, Spain, by 5:55 pm.

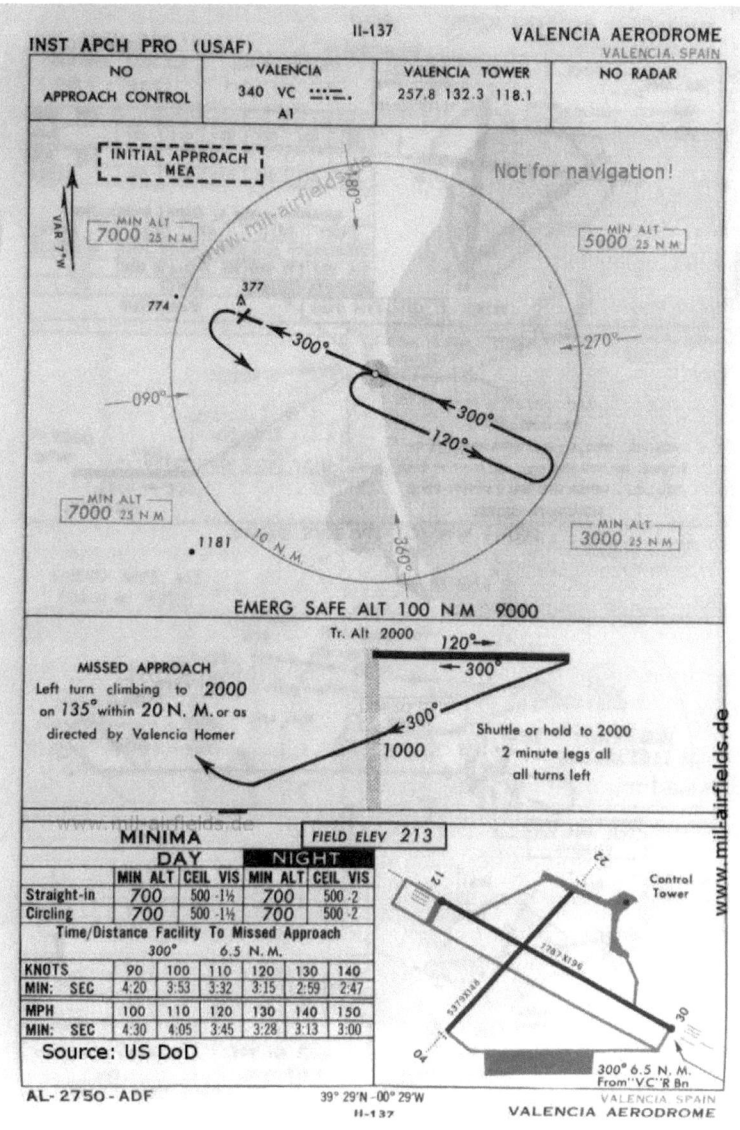

INST APCH PRO (USAF)

VALENCIA AERODROME
VALENCIA, SPAIN

NO APPROACH CONTROL	VALENCIA 340 VC ⸱⸱⸱⸱⸱. A1	VALENCIA TOWER 257.8 132.3 118.1	NO RADAR

INITIAL APPROACH MEA

Not for navigation!

VAR 7°W

MIN ALT 7000 25 NM

MIN ALT 5000 25 NM

377

774°

300°

270°

090°

300°

120°

MIN ALT 7000 25 NM

1181

10 N.M.

360°

MIN ALT 3000 25 NM

EMERG SAFE ALT 100 NM 9000

Tr. Alt 2000

120°

300°

MISSED APPROACH
Left turn climbing to **2000**
on 135° within **20 N. M.** or as
directed by Valencia Homer

300°

1000

Shuttle or hold to 2000
2 minute legs all
all turns left

MINIMA					
	DAY			NIGHT	
	MIN ALT	CEIL VIS	MIN ALT	CEIL VIS	
Straight-in	700	500 -1½	700	500 -2	
Circling	700	500 -1½	700	500 -2	

FIELD ELEV 213

Time/Distance Facility To Missed Approach
300°   6.5 N. M.

KNOTS	90	100	110	120	130	140
MIN: SEC	4:20	3:53	3:32	3:15	2:59	2:47
MPH	100	110	120	130	140	150
MIN: SEC	4:30	4:05	3:45	3:28	3:13	3:00

Source: US DoD

Control Tower

300° 6.5 N. M.
From "VC" R Bn

AL- 2750 - ADF

39° 29'N -00° 29'W
II-137

VALENCIA, SPAIN
VALENCIA AERODROME

Valencia had already been a challenging destination back in 1977 - not due to inadequate facilities, but because the air traffic controllers were either terrible or spoke no English, or they simply didn't understand us.

We planned a radar-guided approach starting over the Mediterranean to the east and heading west on a 300-degree course to Runway 30. The airfield was close to the coast. I flew as "Fortuna 2," in close formation on my leaders right side.

At FL20 (20,000 feet), the Spanish controller directed us:
"Fortuna flight, you are cleared to descend to 5,000 feet, heading 270°."
We began our descent when the controller added,
"Fortuna, you have thunderstorms in front of you."
"We're not flying into that,"
Fortuna lead remarked in German for me.
"We need to descend. The alternate is too far away,"
I cautioned.
"Valencia, Fortuna flight is canceling IFR; we will continue VFR to Valencia."
"Fortuna flight, IFR is canceled. Contact Valencia Tower, 313.8."

The relief in the Spanish controller's voice was palpable, he no longer had to guide us to the airfield using his radar.

Fortuna Lead spiraled us downward, partially through gaps in the clouds and sometimes directly into them. We knew we were over water, so there shouldn't be any obstacles beneath us, unless another aircraft crossed our path. At 5,000 feet, Fortuna Lead began circling to reduce our descent rate. Still, we couldn't see the ground, or, in this situation, the water. As we descended to 2,000 feet, visibility remained nonexistent. At 1,500 feet - nothing. At 1,000 feet, I began to feel uneasy, holding my position at his side. Finally, at 800 feet, we emerged beneath the cloud cover and saw the restless Mediterranean below.

Fortuna Lead set a course toward the airfield, flying low over the water. I checked the TACAN needle, which pointed us directly to the runway, and felt reassured.

"Valencia Tower, Fortuna flight requesting tactical approach to Runway 30."

"Fortuna flight, Valencia Tower. Read you loud and clear, cleared approach for Runway 30. Report three miles out."

The rest was routine. We avoided the thunderstorm, flew low under the clouds to Valencia, and landed. That evening, we enjoyed a bottle of red wine.

The next day, Friday, June 24, 1983, at 8:10 am, we departed Valencia for Málaga - a 470 miles flight along the coast, partially at 5,000 feet and occasionally low-level. Málaga was familiar territory, as described in my chapter "Torremolinos again". The weather there was always good, especially in June. However, for military aircraft was no instrument approach available, and ground radar was unreliable at best. We contacted the tower and received landing clearance.

We prudently requested refueling and oxygen replenishment upon landing, knowing that ground service in Spain generally took longer than in Germany. At NATO airfields, fuel trucks were ready within minutes of engine shutdown, but on civilian airfields in Southern Europe, patience was a virtue. Although Málaga had a military section, it lacked stationed military units. By Monday, we planned to have our aircraft ready to depart without delay.

After filing our flight plan and completing pre-flight inspections, we took off at 10:30 am on June 27 from Málaga-Costa del Sol Airport's Runway 30, heading toward France. Our next stop was Dijon-Longvic (LFSD), home to the "Escadron de Chasse 1/2 Cigognes", equipped with Mirage III-E jets in 1983. Ground service at Dijon was exceptional, as their crews were familiar with Alpha

Jets, which were also flown by the French Air Force. "Cross-servicing" ensured support even for guest aircraft like ours.

Finally, we departed Dijon for our last leg to our home airbase, cruising at FL330/FL350 (33,000–35,000 feet). French air controllers often used foreign military aircraft for intercept exercises, as they did on this flight. Unfortunately, I didn't have my camera ready. A year later, when the Mirage III-E was replaced by the Mirage 2000-C, I managed to capture a photo of a similar intercept exercise in French airspace.

On Monday, June 27, 1983, we landed back at our home airfield, Fürstenfeldbruck.

Mirage 2000C intercepting us at 32,000 feet.

No Jackpot

Sometime in 1985 or 1986, I can't recall the exact year, Germany witnessed its first major lottery jackpot. I believe it was around eleven Million Deutsche Marks, certainly a double-digit Million figures.

We were determined to hit this jackpot and secure our retirement after our flying careers. At least that was the youthful fantasy we had at the time. But how could we participate in the German lottery while living in Portugal?

There was no internet, and even getting a current newspaper in Beja, Portugal was impossible. Often we'd get a paper from the previous day, or even several days old. Satellite television hadn't been invented yet. My preferred daily source of news was "Deutsche Welle" on Short Wave. Frequencies like 6075 kHz or 9095 kHz were standard, with others available during evening or nighttime hours. A "Grundig Satellite 2100 World Receiver" was our connection to Germany, and the world.

We learned about this "Super Jackpot" from the Deutsche Welle news and realized we needed to submit our lottery ticket in Germany by Friday. And why did we have our own Alpha Jets, if not also for such missions?

On a Tuesday, we scheduled a flight from Portugal to Germany for Thursday, with the return the same day. Around six flight hours seemed a reasonable investment for our chance for the Jackpot. Incidentally, our chosen comrade, "voluntarily and in the spirit of camaraderie," of course, could stop by the lottery office in Leipheim (EDSD), home base of the FBW 44, and also pick up various items unavailable in Portugal but much desired by us and our wives.

The list included sausages, sweet mustard, sauerkraut, pantyhose, fresh cold cuts, and the all-important birth control pills from a particular pharmaceutical company, ones not available in

Portugal but most agreeable to our wives. I could easily expand this list by a few pages.

We opted for a system bet, marking "18 numbers out of 49", for about 1,000 DM. The cost was shared among us pilots.

Our selected pilot departed early Thursday morning for Leipheim, investing roughly 1,000 Deutsche Mark of our flight allowances, and returned to Portugal by Thursday evening, just in time for the after-work beers, with a lottery ticket in hand.

All that was left was to wait for Saturday and imagine how we'd enjoy early retirement.

Eighteen numbers out of 49, surely, there had to be "six correct" among them.

As it turned out, every single one of us continued flying to earn our daily bread.

We didn't even manage "three correct numbers." Our winning payout: zero!

My Pilot License was gone

Well, now I have to share the following story, it happened to me in 1985.

After a gunnery mission on "Coca-Range" in Beja, Portugal, I landed on runway 01L. While braking, I noticed a poor braking performance. The brakes didn't respond as usual; they just "slid along," and my taxi speed only slowed enough to exit the runway at the very last taxiway, after 10,000 feet. That was unusual.

The runway, at 10,000 feet, was longer than most military runways, and the Alpha Jet's typical landing roll was a short 2000 feet. This capability made the Alpha Jet well-suited for airfields with shorter runways.

I taxied the aircraft back to the parking area where I had started an hour earlier. As usual, I entered the flight discrepancy in the logbook and noted the inadequate brake performance, recommending a brake inspection. This rendered the aircraft grounded until cleared for flight after an inspection.

The maintenance team brought the jet to the hangar, checked the brake pressure and discs, which had recently been replaced, and found no apparent issues. By the next day, the aircraft was cleared for a "roll test."

When the maintenance team informed me that the jet was ready for a roll test, I immediately decided to conduct the test myself. After all, I clearly remembered the poor braking performance during the previous day's landing.

On my way to the aircraft, our operations NCO asked if he could join me in the rear seat for the roll test. Since this wasn't a flight, the ejection seat would remain locked and armed, making it perfectly safe. Maintenance technicians occasionally joined roll tests in the rear cockpit. So, I agreed:

"Sure."

I started the engines, closed the canopies, and taxied to the runway after getting clearance from the tower for the roll test. I moved to runway 01L, advanced the throttle, accelerated to about 100 knots, then pulled the throttle back to idle and applied the brakes.

The braking performance was unimpressive, just as bad as during the landing. I thought, "Maybe the new brake packs need to be broken in." I requested clearance for another brake test.

Back at the runway threshold of 01L, I again pushed the throttles forward, spooling up the engines and accelerating the jet. At around 60 knots, the airspeed needle moved steadily. At about 100 knots, 10 to 15 knots below the usual landing speed, I pulled the throttles back to idle and applied the brakes. When the aircraft slowed to a brisk walking pace, it came to an abrupt halt, accompanied by a loud "zsssshhh" sound that I could hear even with my helmet on in the cockpit.

What had happened?

During the second "test run", the brake packs overheated so much that the thermal fuses on both tires melted, leaving me with two flat tires. A crane had to be brought in to lift my aircraft using what looked like an oversized belly sling and tow it back to the parking area.

Not only did the tires need replacing, but the wheels and brake packs were also severely damaged, completely burned out from the overheating.

The damage was significant and ultimately led to disciplinary action against me. I lost my pilot's license for one month as punishment because I had disregarded a technical directive.

A year earlier, in Oldenburg (EDNO), a double brake test had ended with glowing brake discs as well. A supplementary directive had been issued in the technical manual stating that brake tests must only involve a single braking attempt. This directive, issued as an "Operational Supplement," had slipped my mind a year later. Forgotten. My fault. Sorry!

For one month, I was confined to "desk flying." To spare me further embarrassment, my squadron commander didn't officially confiscate my pilot's license as required but allowed me to keep it in my possession.

Upon my departure from Beja, Portugal, the "Technical Group" presented me with the burned-out brake disc mounted on a marble plaque as a memento.

Thank you, Gentlemen.

"My" Alpha Jet brake disc.

Near miss

With a right turn, I set course to the south, to the Algarve coast in southern Portugal. Faro was still about a 60 miles ahead of me. To the left of my flight path flowed the Guadiana River, the border between Portugal and Spain in the south of the two countries. That day, I was flying a solo mission on a low-level flight. Normally, we always flew in pairs, sometimes in formations of three or four aircraft. I loved flying solo occasionally. During the four years I spent flying in Portugal, a rich and memorable time, I occasionally arranged solo flights for myself, as I was responsible for planning the training missions.

At 250 feet (75 meters) altitude, I was flying at 360 knots (660 km/h), heading toward the mountain range "Serra do Caldeirão", north of Faro. Above me stretched a gray cloud cover. The sun couldn't break through, and it seemed likely to remain a gray day. Visibility during the low-level flight grew worse the closer I got to the mountain range. It was just barely sufficient for low-level flight. At a speed of 360 knots, the minimum visibility requirement was five kilometers, the distance of 26 seconds of flight time. The visibility was at the minimum, but minutes later, it was starting to even decrease.

I knew the area well, having flown dozens of low-level missions in this southern Alentejo region. I was confident I would find enough cloud gaps to continue on my planned route. Flying solo allowed for great flexibility. In the hills north of the Algarve, I searched for a path through the valleys. I could still vaguely discern the ridges of the higher hills. Occasionally, the cloud cover brushed the hilltops. With 90° banked turns from right to left, I looked for an "exit," descending further into the mountain range and into the next valley.

The valleys became narrower, the hills suddenly seemed taller than they were, and the cloud base kept lowering. Even the smaller hills appeared to grow higher. In one valley, I realized - without a doubt, that there were no gaps left. A 180° turn to fly back wasn't possible anymore without risking crashing into a mountainside.

Trapped in a valley.

My only option was to climb.

So, I leveled the wings, pulled the stick back to my stomach, and ascended through the clouds, aiming for the sun. I knew from the weather briefing that the cloud layer was continuous but not particularly thick. I would pop out of the clouds, cork-like, at around 360 miles per hour. This maneuver was my last option to escape the terrain under these weather conditions. Such a "last-ditch maneuver" had served as my "emergency brake" more than once in my flying career.

It grew gray around me; the clouds enveloped my aircraft entirely. I pushed the throttle fully forward - full power - switching my focus between the artificial horizon, altimeter, and airspeed indicator, while waiting to see the sun appear in my upper field of vision.

The clouds grew brighter, and two or three seconds later, I burst through them, cork-like - and saw the plane in front of me.

TAP Lockheed _L-1011 TriStar.

The belly of a TAP (Transportes Aéreos Portugueses) Lockheed L-1011 TriStar. Its landing gear extended, it was on approach to Faro Airport and seconds from entering the clouds to deliver hundreds of tourists to the beach. In an instant, I yanked the control stick back into my stomach, pulling the nose of my aircraft above the L-1011 TriStar fuselage to avoid flying through it. The L-1011 TriStar, with its 440-seat capacity, was nearly the size of a Jumbo Jet.

A second later, I was about 100 feet above the L-1011 TriStar. I rolled my plane inverted and watched as it disappeared into the clouds. I then lowered my aircraft's nose through the inverted position to descend quickly through a gap in the clouds, returning to low-level flight and continuing my mission.

The Portuguese radar didn't detect my plane, and no one noticed my "encounter." Later, while searching online, I found a photo of the three-engined TAP L-1011 TriStar. It must have been "that exact aircraft" in the photo, after all, to my knowledge, TAP only operated two L-1011 TriStar in its fleet.

After that flight, I never again entered clouds from low-level flight uncontrollably. From then on, I made the decision to abort low-level flights due to deteriorating weather conditions much earlier.

JaboG 44 - Active on Request

The FBW 44 was previously known as LeKG 44, the "Light Fighter Bomber Wing 44," equipped with the Fiat G.91 "Gina." From a former radar controller stationed in Leipheim, the then base of LeKG 44, I received two unusual and rare photographs of the G.91 from that era.

G.91 "Gina" in the 60s.

Note the old designation EC+108; the "EC" identification was reassigned in 1962 to Recce Wing 53. This reconnaissance squadron was established in Erding on October 1, 1960, relocated to Leipheim in 1962, and renamed "Leichtes Kampfgeschwader 44." Its role as a pure reconnaissance squadron ended with its restructuring on June 1, 1965. From then, the squadron's mission shifted to "Light Combat Squadron" with a focus on "Close Air Support."

On June 1, 1975, just 13 years after its formation, LeKG 44 was disbanded. In 1981, a concept emerged, initially as a written order, to establish an "Air Force Reserve Squadron." Using the 18 Alpha Jet aircraft from Beja Airbase, personnel, and reservists, the idea was to form an additional "Squadron" for wartime. Leipheim Airbase, which housed an Alpha Jet maintenance facility, was operational as an Air Force Airbase, and a suitable location.

For the first time in 1983, the JaboG 44(GE) - "GE" standing for "Geräteeinheit" (equipment unit), was activated using aircraft, pilots, and technicians from the Tactical Training Command in Beja, Portugal, along with reservist pilots maintaining their operational status. This created a reinforced squadron. From September 12 to 23, 1983, the first activation exercise took place. Subsequent reactivation were planned to occur biennially as part of the "Heller Blitz" exercise.

On September 7, 1985, we took off from Beja, Portugal in three-aircraft formations and relocated to Leipheim. The Tactical Training Command in Beja would provided 10 out of 18 aircraft for the activation exercise, with three additional aircraft deployed from FBW 49 in Fürstenfeldbruck for reinforcement. In practice, Alpha Jets from all Alpha Jet units were gathered on the flight line for use in the exercise. In a coincidental lineup captured in a photo, aircraft from different units stood side by side, showcasing the collective effort.

On September 11, 1985, the weather in Leipheim was marginal, just sufficient for takeoff. The forecast for the route to Army Training Area Grafenwöhr was rated as "adequate," and the target area was predicted to have a low cloud base. At the Grafenwöhr training area, a substantial audience, including high-ranking officers with silver and golden stars on their shoulders, awaited an impressive display of weapons deployment.

Our mission, communicated the night before via an Air Task Order, involved preparing an attack with 2.75 FFAR unguided rockets on a ground target at the training area. After a joint briefing, where the unfavorable weather report was discussed, we moved to the navigation room to plan our mission. In a four-aircraft "Card Four Formation," we flew low-level through Nördlingen, between Nuremberg and Neumarkt in der Oberpfalz, heading toward Grafenwöhr. Each aircraft carried two rocket pods under its wings, each loaded with 19 rockets.

Alpha Jets from 4 different FBW.

During the low-level flight, the wingmen maintained positions based on visibility, sometimes a mile apart, which was optimal, and sometimes much closer to avoid losing sight of the leader due to low-hanging clouds. Repeatedly, we had to leave our designated 500-foot altitude to find gaps in the clouds. Southwest of Grafenwöhr, we contacted a Forward Air Controller (FAC) by radio. The weather report indicated five kilometers of visibility and a cloud base between 1,500 and 5,000 feet. For our attack, we needed at least a 4,500-foot cloud ceiling to fire the rockets at a 20-degree angle. A shallower angle would result in greater dispersion, making it impossible to comply with safety zones on tightly regulated ranges in peacetime.

Orders were precise:
"Dice flight, second element, take two minutes spacing."
"WILCO."
"Dice flight push."

The pilots in all four aircraft pushed the throttles to 98% power, accelerating to 400 knots attack speed.

We remained just below the low cloud ceiling, aware that finding a gap large enough for the target approach would be a gamble, especially so close to the grandstand. Positioned to the right of "Dice Lead", I focused entirely on maintaining formation, as navigation to the target was now the leader's responsibility.

At the Initial Point (IP), "Dice Lead" turned slightly upward toward the target. The apex,

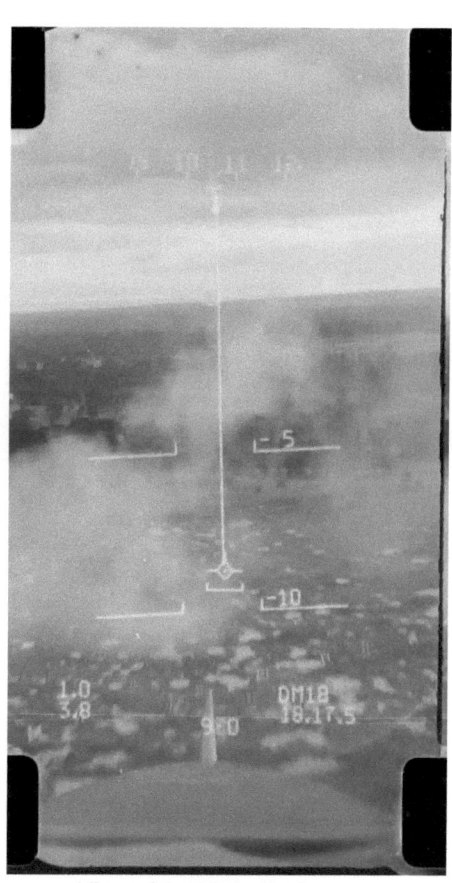

View of the Head Up Display.

245

calculated at 4,500 feet, was never reached below the cloud ceiling. Nevertheless, we initiated the attack in close formation.

"Dice lead element, pickle, pickle - now!"

The "pickle button" released 38 rockets from my aircraft, all aimed at the designated ground target.

After firing, we pulled out of the attack with 4g into a left turn. I fell slightly behind the leader, making it easier to maintain formation and scan the airspace for potential threats. In my 10 o'clock position, I saw the spectators on the grandstand and the ground setup for the exercise.

Intense weapons deployment with Matra 250kg. Weapons 'for the enemy' were often marked with messages by the weapons technicians, and this Matra bomb was also signed by 'Franzl'.

The second element, "Dice Three" and "Dice Four," also successfully delivered their rockets, completing the mission. Minutes later, we were back in tactical formation, flying low-level toward home base.

Our mission - a "close-air-support" demonstration - had been a success. From the ground, the Army Officers and Generals had no perception of the regulatory limits we had pushed due to the low-hanging clouds.

"Franzl".

Alpha Jet with rocket-pods for 19 unguided rockets.

Barf bag

"Today, we're flying to the Black Forest," I explained to the doctor of Institute for Aerospace Medicine, who leaned against the counter in the operations room of our squadron, wearing a red flight suit without a name tag or insignia to indicate his affiliation. He had been announced to me as today's "ride-along." Finally, the doctor was about to experience the "depths of aviation," as he himself contributed to the evaluation of flight suitability for pilots and aircrew in the German Air Force. Most of our flight surgeons were well-regarded because they were "on our side" as much as regulations allowed.

One well-known flight surgeon was Dr. B., whom I knew from our shared time at the Airborne and Air Transport School in Altenstadt. For 18 months, I had been assigned to lead the survival training for Luftwaffe aircrews. A lighthearted anecdote from that time is worth sharing:

All the Army Officers had assembled in the "Tower Hall" for "Army Tactical Training." As a young First Lieutenant in the Luftwaffe, I had been ordered to attend but was not given any specific role like company or platoon leader. I was merely an observer.

The tactics' instructor was presenting the "Friendly Forces Situation" and was just about to outline their mission when he paused for two or three seconds. His face turned beet red as he looked toward the farthest corner of the room. Then, in a sharp, commanding tone, he shouted, "That applies to you too, Dr. B.!"

About fifty officers turned their heads to the far corner, where she, the flight surgeon sat, knitting needles in hand, clearly disinterested in the "tactical situation" of the companies and battalions. She was knitting!

"Yes, knitting," with a ball of yarn resting on her uniform skirt, she replied: "Queen Juliana of the Netherlands also knits during the opening of Parliament."

I don't know if Queen Juliana actually knitted during parliamentary openings, but whether true or not, it was a brilliant provocation.

Back to my story. I took the senior flight surgeon from the Air Force's Aerospace Medical Institute to the large navigation table and outlined the route for our flight. It was a low-level flight past the Swabian Alps, heading west to Freudenstadt, then south to the dam of the Schluchsee Reservoir, and finally eastward back home to "Fürsty" (Fürstenfeldbruck). The "doctor" explained that while he was theoretically familiar with aviation, he lacked "hands-on experience," which he intended to gain today.

Over the years, I had occasionally taken passengers on flights in the G.91 or Alpha Jet two-seaters. I always aimed to provide them with an unforgettable, positive experience. Preparing a passenger for their first ride took significant time, as I had to teach them essential emergency procedures to avoid dangerous mistakes under stress. The highlight of the pre-flight briefing was always this line:

"If we need to eject, I'll yell 'Bail out, bail out, bail out.' If you're still sitting in your seat after the third 'Bail out,' you'll be flying solo because I'll already be hanging from my parachute."

It was said in jest, but it never failed to make an impression.

The Alpha Jet had a "command bail-out system." If either the pilot or the back seater pulled the ejection handle, the rear seat would eject first, followed 0.4 seconds later by the front seat. Some pilots disabled this automatic mode for passenger flights, reasoning, "I won't let a panicked passenger eject me and crash my plane."

I completely agreed with that sentiment.

During the pre-flight briefing, a squadron mate pulled me aside and told me: "That jerk from the Aerospace Medical Institute denied my wife a flight ride." He was referring to a flight approval request similar to one granted to a civilian, Mrs. Strubel, in 1979. Her request had been approved by the Secretary of Defense.

Now, that same flight surgeon who denied the request was my passenger. It was his first ride in a Fighter Plane.

"Show him what it's like to fly in a combat aircraft," my squadron mate suggested with a mischievous grin.

Thirty minutes later, we were strapped into our ejection seats and airborne. Cruising at 360 knots, I began narrating my thoughts to give the doctor insight into the decision-making process during flight.

"In the two o'clock position, there's a small village. We'll stay a mile left of it...time check, 4:45 minutes, on track... tower at eleven o'clock, small town ahead; we'll bypass it to the left, 6:20 minutes, looking good..."

At first, the doctor responded to each of my observations, but as the flight progressed, his replies became less frequent. About 30 minutes in, he fell silent.

As we entered the rolling hills of the Black Forest, turbulence intensified. The doctor's breathing grew rapid and labored. Suddenly, I heard a loud hiss through the cockpit. He had removed his oxygen mask. I glanced in the rearview mirror.

"Still with me?" I asked.

No response.

Then came a faint sound: "Chrchrchrchr..."

"I think I'm getting sick," he muttered.

At that moment, I banked the aircraft sharply, pulling 5g. If a passenger felt nauseous, I sometimes distracted them with a trick:

"Look! There's a police accident down there, three cars with flashing lights." Passengers would search for the imaginary scene, forgetting their nausea.

But I refrained from using that trick on the doctor.

As we began our simulated attack on the Schluchsee dam, I noticed the doctor was entirely unresponsive, save for faint hissing sounds and occasional retching.

When we completed the flight and landed in Lechfeld due to a runway delay at Fürsty, the doctor staggered out of the jet, clutching a full vomit bag in one hand. His face was pale, and he refused my offer for a coffee.

On the return flight, the turbulence had eased, but his silence remained. His first and last flight in a combat aircraft was certainly unforgettable - for both of us.

Last Backseat Ride

During my active duty, I never had the opportunity to fly as a back seater in an F-4F Phantom II. The legendary "Phantom" would occasionally cross my path, but the chance simply never presented itself.

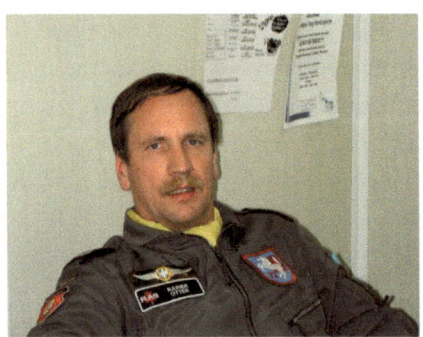

Years later, as a reservist assigned to FW 72 "Westfalen" as an S-2 Intel (intelligence staff officer), I asked about the possibility of flying in a Phantom. The commander, to whom I posed the question, hesitated for only a moment before replying: "You know that's not possible, and it's against regulations." He added, "You also don't have a Red Card anymore."

The "Red Card" from the Air Force's Aerospace Medical Institute certified participation in flight medical training and a "flight" in the hypobaric chamber. This certification was valid for only three years and required regular renewal. Without a valid Red Card, no flights in combat aircraft were allowed, not even for VIPs, flight

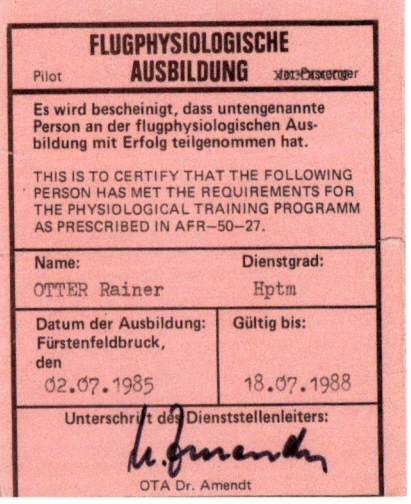

surgeons, air traffic controllers, or the famous case of Mrs. Strubel[37].

Months went by. I continued my assignments with the squadron, mostly during routine squadron exercises or Tactical Evaluations (TacEval), preparing for NATO readiness assessments.

In 2001, the squadron leadership invited me to serve as an intelligence staff officer for "Exercise Maple Flag" in Cold Lake, Canada, the second-largest Air Force exercise in the world. The Luftwaffe participated with six F-4F Phantoms and six MiG-29s.

After the exercise officially concluded, the pilots used the remaining days before returning to Germany to perform low-level flights at 100 feet. In the Canadian Air Force's restricted area, neither altitude nor speed was limited.

I was speaking with our German Commander in the operations center when I overheard the operations officer asking: "Who else is flying in the 4-ship?"

My response was spontaneous:

"Me."

The Commander looked at me in surprise, and I asked, "May I join?"

He thought for a few seconds - longer than his predecessor had years ago in Hopsten - and answerd:

"Okay."

Two hours later, I was strapped into the backseat of an F-4F Phantom.

Call Sign: "Rhino."
Takeoff: 12:00 pm.
Planned flight time: 1 hour and 10 minutes.

In the backseat of 38+03

Coincidentally, the pilot in the front seat was the son of one of my former flight instructors on the Fiat G.91 in Fürsty.

Eight of us left the squadron building and drove together in a crew van to our aircraft on the flight line. All the German F-4Fs were lined up, ready for the mission. The crews performed their walk-around checks and climbed into their cockpits. The "Before-Engine-Start Check" were completed quickly, and the engines were started.

Then came the "Pre-Taxi Check."

"Cold Lake Tower, Rhino four F-4s taxi," our lead called to the control tower.

"Good morning, Rhino. Taxi to Runway 31R," the tower replied. "Wind 280 at 12 knots, QNH 1021."

"Runway 31R...good morning," our lead confirmed.

The four F-4Fs taxied to the runway, a short distance from our parking position. Shortly before reaching the runway, we heard: "Cold Lake Tower, Rhino requests takeoff."

"Rhino, cleared for takeoff. Report leaving the control zone."

Our four F-4Fs rolled into position on the 12,600-foot runway. During the "Before Takeoff Check," the J-79 engines were brought to 100% power (military power), held in place by the brakes. The thrust caused the nose gear to compress slightly, and the vibrations of the aircraft could be felt.

Our lead looked over his shoulder at the other three aircraft and received a nod from each pilot, signaling that the checks were completed, and all planes were ready.

"Rhino Lead" began rolling. Eight seconds later, my front-seater released the brakes and pushed the throttle levers from "Mil Power" all the way forward to the Afterburner.

The acceleration that followed is indescribable to anyone who hasn't flown in a Fighter Jet, it's breathtaking. The F-4F, lightly loaded with only a centerline fuel tank, accelerated like a Porsche on a racetrack. Our jet followed "Rhino 1" at an eight-second interval. At rotation speed, the pilot raised the nose 12° above the horizon, and the aircraft lifted off, quickly accelerating to 420 knots.

Flying an F-4F without external tanks, or just with a centerline tank, is every fighter pilot's dream. The twin J-79 engines deliver raw, brutal power.

After 1 hour and 10 minutes, we landed back at Cold Lake.
I will always remember my final flight in a Luftwaffe Fighter Plane as a gift, a fitting tribute to my years "in the cockpit."

Low-level flight in Canada - Cold Lake, June 22, 2001.

Afghanistan

Between 2005 and 2007, I spent nearly eleven months deployed in Afghanistan.

Flying on the tail ramp of a CH-47 "Chinook"

Four of those months were as an "Intelligence Branch Chief" with the Multinational Brigade in Kabul; the remainder was spent with OEF - "Operation Enduring Freedom," or the "War on Terror," as it was referred to by U.S. Forces. German media almost exclusively reported on the ISAF mission, avoiding the word "War," despite the undeniable combat situations in some regions of Afghanistan. The term was taboo until Germany's former Secretary of Defense, Karl-Theodor zu Guttenberg, described the deployment as a "war-like situation."

We were all acutely aware of the risks involved in our deployment and did not look shy away from them when duty required. However, I observed in Kabul, that a few soldiers, and even fewer officers, actively sought to avoid any personal risk if they could find a way around it.

For the last six months of my deployment, I served as the German Liaison Officer (LNO) at the U.S. Headquarter in Bagram, approximately 60 km north of Kabul. Our accommodations were located directly across from the infamous "Detention Facility," where Taliban fighters were detained and "extensively" interrogated. We were never provided with further details and weren't expected to ask. Among U.S. soldiers, it was unofficially referred to as the "Guantanamo of Afghanistan."

To fulfill my responsibilities as expected, I frequently accompanied U.S. troops, traveling either in armored vehicles or aboard supply helicopters.

One of our destinations was Camp Blessing, located in Kunar Province. A U.S. CH-47 Chinook was conducting a supply run, and I took the opportunity to join the flight to gain firsthand insight into the security situation in the area.

I was offered a seat next to the "tail gunner" on the open tail ramp. Accompanied by two Apache attack helicopters, we flew low into Kunar Province, heading toward the remote camp near the Pakistani border. Camp Blessing was a U.S. outpost under constant attack from the Taliban.

Our three-helicopter formation flew low, taking advantage of the hilly terrain and the mountainous northeastern region for tactical cover. The objective was to minimize the time a potential enemy, including the several independent terror groups in the region, would have to react to the helicopters presence. Likely threats included AK-47s, 12.7mm DShK machine guns, SA-7 Grails, and even Stingers.

The two Apache helicopters vigilantly scanned the ground along our flight path, ready to return fire immediately if attacked and to neutralize Taliban or any other hostile forces targeting us.

The photo shows how every homestead and garden represented a potential threat to the door gunners.

The landscape was harsh and inhospitable, barren hills resembling a lunar surface. Minutes would pass without a single tree or shrub in sight. Only along the edges of streams and rivers did green gardens appear, signaling life. These were places where people were always present, often watching the helicopters intently.

The expressions and gestures of those on the ground varied: some appeared frightened, others hostile. Their faces showed either indifference or anger, nothing in between. This stark reality underscored the constant danger in Afghanistan: death could await around any corner or behind any rock.

Sitting beside the tail gunner on the lowered ramp, my feet dangled in the slipstream behind and below the helicopter.

Suddenly, the tail gunner fired to the right and downward. My eyes followed the direction of the machine gun's barrel, catching the muzzle flashes of gunfire from a walled compound aimed in our direction, narrowly missing us.

The Apache trailing to our right veered toward the identified threat, engaging the enemy on the ground, who continued firing at us. I saw the short muzzle flashes of the adversary and the telltale smoke clouds from the Apache's cannon. Within ten seconds, the encounter was over.

This incident was a stark reminder of how often life and death in a deployment are decided in mere moments.

Luck always plays a part.

Camp Blessing in Afghanistan

Flight line Party

"Pilots Corner" in the Officer's Club at "Fürsty."

The "Flight Line Party" is one of the oldest traditional events of the German Air Force. Held annually at the Officer's Club in Fürstenfeldbruck, the party has long been a highlight for many former aviators, a cherished occasion for reunions, reminiscing, and a Gentlemen's evening of a unique kind.

I feel it is time to mention this place, the Bar, where all Luftwaffe fighter pilots have stood at some point, because the future of the "Flight Line Party" is uncertain. If "Fürsty airfield" is indeed fully abandoned by 2026, this place will be lost for us pilots, forever.

Traditionally, the gathering took place once a year, always on the Thursday before Christmas week. Invitations were extended - and will continue until what may be the final "Flight Line Party" - to all pilots who served at the airbase of Fürstenfeldbruck. This includes those stationed there from the handover of the airbase by the USAF to the German Air Force on November 1, 1957, to the disbandment of Fighter-Bomber Wing 49 in 1994.

Those who remember the wild parties of the 1970s and 1980s described in the chapter "Fighter Pilots Parties" will recognize that the "Flight Line Party" has always been a more dignified gathering of former pilots.

The wild parties are history now, but the hours spent in the air, in the squadrons, or at the bar remain vivid in our memories, and in mine as well. That's why I've taken the time to write down my experiences.

Not everyone experienced them the same way I did. Some of my comrades may remember "Wild Parties", while others experienced things more modestly.

Not everyone has to appreciate these moments, nor must they share them. These are my lived memories.

The pilots who played tag with their own shadows in cumulus clouds, who chased their own contrails, without saying a word about it afterward, but can still recall those impressions 30 years later, as if they had just happened that morning, those pilots will understand exactly what I mean.

Afterburner!

While browsing through classic aviation literature, an Aviation Cocktail makes for a fitting drink.

The original recipe for the Aviation Cocktail was first published in 1916 in Hugo Ensslin's recipe collection "Recipes for Mixed Drinks".

German-born Hugo Ensslin was a bartender at the "Wallick Hotel" on New York's Times Square at the time. Ensslin is credited as the inventor of the Aviation Cocktail.

No Last Word

Fighter Pilots!

Images of "Maverick" from Top Gun, or elite aerobatic teams like the Red Arrows, Thunderbirds, or Frecce Tricolori instantly come to mind. Dozens of books have been written, and breathtaking films produced all portraying the courage, composure, recklessness, and undeniable charm of these audacious "heroes" in their Fighter Jets.

But there is another side to being a fighter pilot. Not every mission is a cinematic dogfight.

In this collection of short stories, the author takes us beyond the glamour and into the often-overlooked daily life of a young pilot. From his first flight training in the United States to his years of service in various squadrons, he recounts the small, unvarnished moments that shaped his journey, as a Second Lieutenant, Lieutenant, and eventually a Captain.

These anecdotes offer a rare glimpse into the routines, mishaps and quiet triumphs behind the spotlight; stories that have rarely, if ever, been told.

Accompanied by eighty personal photographs, this intimate book opens a window onto the life of a jet pilot during the 1970s and 1980s, behind the scenes, beyond the myths, and deeply human.

Loved life,
Kissed sin,
Gave our hearts to women.
And yet never flinched
when death greeted us
That is a pilot's life.

Manfred Freiherr von Richthofen

Acknowledgements

With deep respect and heartfelt gratitude, I dedicate these lines to my fellow aviators, to whom I entrusted my life in critical moments. Through storm and cloud, high and low, they flew steadfastly also at my side until we once again stood together on solid ground. The joy we shared during our celebrations, often in the company of our Allied friends, remains etched in memory.

My sincere thanks also go to my friend Ruby from New York City, a native English speaker, who inspired me to make my experiences as a fighter pilot in the German Air Force during the 1970s and 80s accessible to English-speaking readers. Her tireless support made this book possible. Without Ruby, it would never have seen the light of day.

About the Author

Born in 1954, in Aschaffenburg, he grew up on his parents farm in a small village named Winzenhohl. Agriculture, a poultry farm, the volunteer fire department, and his time as an altar boy shaped his childhood.

At the age of fourteen, he obtained his first driver's license for tractors and completed an agricultural apprenticeship to take over the family business.

He later earned a secondary school diploma through a non-traditional educational

Photo: Nicola di Nuncio 1987.

path and became a fighter pilot in the Air Force.